Study Guide

Social Psychology and Human Nature

Roy F. Baumeister
Florida State University

Brad J. Bushman
University of Michigan

Prepared by

Kristin Beals
California State University, Fullerton

THOMSON
WADSWORTH

Australia • Brazil • Canada • Mexico • Singapore • Spain • United Kingdom • United States

Printed in the United States of America

1 2 3 4 5 6 7 11 10 09 08 07

Printer: Thomson West

ISBN-13: 978-0-534-63836-8
ISBN-10: 0-534-63836-8

Thomson Higher Education
10 Davis Drive
Belmont, CA 94002-3098
USA

For more information about our products, contact us at:
Thomson Learning Academic Resource Center
1-800-423-0563

Table of Contents

Preface

This study guide was written for Baumeister and Bushman's *Social Psychology and Human Nature*. Prepared by Kristin Beals, California State University–Fullerton, each chapter of this Study Guide includes a review, a test, suggested readings, and an answer key. Each chapter review is organized around the major sections of the chapter and includes

- Snapshot: A one- or two-sentence overview of that particular section.
- Learning Objectives: Statements that explain what a student should be able to understand or be able to do after mastering that section.
- Understanding the Terminology: A matching exercise based on the key terms for that section.
- Summary: A brief summary formatted as a fill-in-the blank exercise.

Each chapter test covers all the major sections of the chapter and includes

- multiple-choice questions
- true-false questions
- short essay questions

The suggested readings present additional resources that you could consult for additional information. You may be able to find these resources at your school library.

After the chapters, the Study Guide also contains questions related to the Application Modules, which can be found at the end of many textbooks.

For additional study aids, be sure to log on to the **companion website** for Social Psychology and Human Nature at www.thomsonedu.com/psychology/baumeister

Also consider **ThomsonNow**, the robust online study and learning tool, available for purchase. This online resource can help you gauge your own unique study needs. A Pre-Test helps you identify what you need to study more—you receive your score automatically. Based on your results, you receive a Personalized Study plan that outlines the concepts you need to review. Working from your Personalized Study plan, you are guided to visual images, video exercises with questions, learning modules and animations, and other resources to help you master the material. For more information about **ThomsonNow**, visit www.thomsonedu.com/psychology

CHAPTER 1 – THE MISSION AND THE METHOD

CHAPTER REVIEW

Section 1: A Brief History of Social Psychology

Snapshot

Social Psychology got its start in the late 1800s, but really came into its own in the 1950s and 1960s. Two important early ideas that helped the field develop was Allport's focus on attitudes and Lewin's idea that the person interacts with the situation to predict behavior.

Learning Objectives

- Describe the work of the two earliest researchers in social psychology.
- Explain the major issues or focus of each period of social psychological history.
- Describe how behaviorism, Freudian psychoanalysis and social psychology relate to one another.

Summary

Use the appropriate terms to complete each summary.

1. An early study conducted by ____________________, examined whether children reeled fishing lines faster or slower when with other children. He found that children were __________________ when with other children.

2. Two different camps of thought were very important in forming social psychology. _________________ is an approach to explaining behavior through principles of reward and punishment. _______________________ is an approach that looks to deep unconscious forces inside the person to explain behavior.

Section 2: What do Social Psychologists Do?

Snapshot

Social Psychology is the study of how our affect, behavior, and cognitions are influenced by the real or imagined presence of other people.

Learning Objective

- ❖ Define social psychology and explain the ABC triad.

Summary

Use the appropriate terms to complete each summary.

1. Social psychologist study the "ABC's," where A refers to ________________, B refers to ________________ , and C refers to ______________ .

Section 3: Social Psychology's Place in the World

Snapshot

Social psychology is a part of the social sciences along with anthropology, economics, history, political science, and sociology. Social Psychology is unique among the areas of psychology because of its focus on studying how the social situation effects thoughts, feelings, and behaviors.

Learning Objectives

- ❖ Explain how anthropology, economics, history, political science, and sociology differ in their focus on different aspects of social life.
- ❖ Explain how social psychology is different from and intertwined with biological psychology, clinical psychology, cognitive psychology, developmental psychology, and personality psychology.

Understanding Terminology

Match the terms on the right to the definitions/examples on the left.

______ 1. Likely to study the culture of the Inuit people.	a. anthropology
______ 2. Likely to study if it is easier to remember names or places.	b. economics
______ 3. Likely to study the changing views in our society.	c. history
______ 4. Likely to study how the shortage of fuel oil effects prices.	d. political science
______ 5. Likely to study neurons in the brain.	e. sociology
______ 6. Likely to study the changing government in Iraq.	f. biological psychology
______ 7. Likely to study the mental disorder of schizophrenia.	g. clinical psychology
______ 8. Likely to study the development of motor skills in children.	h. cognitive psychology
______ 9. Likely to study the U.S. Civil War.	i. developmental psychology
______ 10. Likely to study authoritarian personality.	j. personality psychology

Summary

Use the appropriate terms to complete each summary.

1. Anthropology and economics are both ______________________ . Clinical psychology and developmental psychology are both branches of ________________ . Social psychology shares many similarities and differences with the other social sciences and branches of psychology.

Section 4: Why People Study Social Psychology

Snapshot

There are a number of different reasons that people are drawn to social psychology including curiosity about people, a love of wisdom, a desire to make the world a better place, and because it is FUN!

Learning Objective

- ❖ Describe the reasons for studying social psychology.

Summary

Use the appropriate terms to complete each summary.

1. ___________________ differs from ___________________ because it relies on deep and systematic thinking about questions instead of on using the ___________________.

2. Social psychologists who are working to solve real-word problems such as violence, pollution, and prejudice are engaged in ___________________.

Section 5: How do Social Psychologists Answer Their Own Questions?

Snapshot

Social psychologists rely on the scientific method to test hypotheses often derived from theories. Researchers use both experimental and non-experimental studies to test hypotheses. Both types of studies have their own strengths and weaknesses.

Learning Objectives

- ❖ Explain what the relation is between accumulated common wisdom and social psychological research.
- ❖ Describe the scientific method.
- ❖ Describe the place of scientific theories in social psychology.
- ❖ Explain the research designs used by social psychologists including defining independent variable, dependent variable, experiment, random assignment, quasi-experiment, internal validity, field experiment, and external validity.
- ❖ Contrast experimental realism and mundane realism.
- ❖ Describe the correlation approach.

Understanding Terminology

Match the terms on the right to the definitions/examples on the left.

______ 1. "Happiness will be positively associated with frequency of contact with friends."	a. experiment
______ 2. Able to generalize to other samples.	b. independent variable
______ 3. An example would be an experiment conducted on a playground.	c. reactance
______ 4. Manipulating one variable to see if it causes change in another.	d. correlation coefficient
______ 5. Is the D.V. a good representation of the construct?	e. hypothesis
______ 6. Every participant has an equal chance of being assigned to a level of the I.V.	f. correlational approach
______ 7. The variable that is supposed to be effected by the I.V.	g. construct validity of the cause
______ 8. A person who is part of the research team but plays the part of a participant.	h. external validity
______ 9. The variable that is manipulated in an experiment.	i. random assignment
______ 10. "The amount of ice cream consumed is associated with the number of murders."	j. theories
______ 11. Manipulation of the I.V. is the cause of changes in the D.V.	k. internal validity
______ 12. A study in which the I.V. cannot be randomly assigned (e.g., gender).	l. mundane realism
______ 13. The independent variable is operationalized appropriately.	m. field experiment
______ 14. "r = .23" is an example.	n. operational definition
______ 15. The experiment "looks" like the real world.	o. quasi-experiment
______ 16. Observing variables to see if they are associated with one another.	p. confederate
______ 17. Ideas that are linked together in a logical way.	q. dependent variable
______ 18. Behavior exhibited in response to others trying to constrain behavior.	r. correlation
______ 19. The experiment "feels" like the real world.	s. construct validity of the effect
______ 20. Turning the I.V. and D.V. into constructs that can be observed.	t. experimental realism

Summary

Use the appropriate terms to complete each summary.

1. __________________ are composed of abstract ideas or concepts that are linked together and should help us understand human behavior, thoughts, and feelings. A __________________ is a specific prediction.

2. In Dr. Rennard's study on chicken soup and the common cold, the independent variable was __________________ and the dependent variable was __________________. If this were an __________________, participants would be __________________ to either receive a bowl of soup or to receive no soup. If the researchers had simply observed whether participants ate chicken soup on their own and how long their cold symptoms lasted, the researchers would have been taking the __________________ approach.

Section 6: How Much of Social Psychology is True?

Snapshot

Social psychology, like other sciences, is a study in progress that is self-correcting as it builds on past research. Social psychologists are also cautious about generalizing when their research is conducted primarily on college students and individuals from Western cultures.

Learning Objectives

- Describe how mistakes in science are corrected.
- Explain the potential effect of reliance on student samples and culture on research findings.

Summary

Use the appropriate terms to complete each summary.

1. Through __________________ social psychology finds and corrects erroneous conclusions. Social psychological research has been criticized for relying too heavily on __________________ for research participants. This may hinder the __________________ of some findings.

CHAPTER TEST

Multiple Choice Questions

1. Dr. Tomatsu believes that behavior can be understood by asking deep questions about a person's past feelings and thoughts. Which of the following camps does Dr. Tomatsu likely subscribe to?
   a. dream analysis
   b. behaviorism
   c. evolutionary psychology
   d. Freudian psychoanalysis

2. Gordon Allport was an important early contributor to social psychology because
   a. he claimed attitudes were important and useful.
   b. he began to think about biology.
   c. he said behavior is a function of the person and situation.
   d. he invented the term self-esteem.

3. Affect is to feelings as cognition is to
   a. actions.
   b. thoughts.
   c. behaviors.
   d. the brain.

4. Which of the following branches of psychology has the strongest ties to social psychology?
   a. clinical
   b. personality
   c. developmental
   d. biological

5. Dr. Pierre Dumont is researching the recycling patterns of urban areas with the hope that his research will increase the percentage of garbage that is recycled. What type of research is he doing?
   a. basic
   b. evolutionary
   c. developmental
   d. applied

6. Social psychologists set their significance level at .05. What does this mean?
   a. Studies will produce significant results less than 5% of the time.
   b. Studies will produce significant results more than 5% of the time.
   c. Researchers can be 95% confident that their results represent a real difference.
   d. Researchers can be 5% confident that their results are not a fluke.

7. Researchers studying helping want to know if people are more willing to help a stranger if the stranger is a man or a woman. In this set-up, what is the dependent variable?
a. helping
b. gender of stranger
c. gender of participant
d. the stranger

8. Dr. Mendez is interested in studying how having others like us makes us feel good about ourselves. He set up a study in which a confederate enters the waiting area where there is a participant "waiting" for the study to begin. In fact, the study is already happening as the confederate interacts with the participant in the waiting room. Half of the participants are spoken to by the confederate in a very friendly manner and are complimented and asked for lunch. The other half of the participants are spoken to by the confederate but only about the weather that day. Hidden cameras capture how much the participant smiles. If smiling is a good indicator of feeling good about ourselves, we would say the study has
a. internal validity.
b. external validity.
c. construct validity of the cause.
d. construct validity of the effect.

9. If the first ten participants to show up to the study are assigned to the experimental group and the next ten participants are assigned to the control group, there is a failure of
a. the theory.
b. random assignment.
c. mundane realism.
d. experimental realism.

10. Which of the following methods would be ideal for studying the relationship between attitudes toward global warming and gender?
a. a case study
b. a field experiment
c. a quasi-experiment
d. correlational approach

11. If a researcher, who is interested in studying how people react to different styles of communication from a doctor, redecorates her laboratory to physically look as much like a doctor's office as possible, she is working on having good
    a. mundane realism.
    b. experimental realism.
    c. validity.
    d. reliability.

12. What can a correlation between X and Y be interpreted to mean?
    a. X causes Y
    b. Y causes X
    c. some other variable causes X and Y
    d. all of the above

13. Which of the following correlations shows the weakest association between two variables?
    a. r = .67
    b. r = - .34
    c. r = .12
    d. r = - 17

14. In Dr. Rennard's study of the effects of chicken soup on cold symptoms, what did he find?
    a. Chicken soup was only helpful if it contained vegetables with a lot of vitamin C.
    b. People were actually more congested after eating hot soup.
    c. People were less congested after eating hot soup.
    d. Hot soup had no effect on symptoms.

15. Researchers have most often studied
    a. college students.
    b. people from Western societies.
    c. older people.
    d. a and b.

16. If a participant becomes psychologically absorbed in the study and it "feels" real, the study is said to have high
    a. mundane realism.
    b. psychological reactance.
    c. experimental realism.
    d. demand characteristics.

17. Internal validity refers to the extent
    a. in which changes in the independent variable caused changes in the dependent variable.
    b. in which the finding from the study can be generalized to other people.
    c. that the study followed the scientific method.
    d. which the internal states of the participants reflect what would happen in the real world.

18. If a researcher, who wanted to know how distracting noises effects test taking, sets up an experiment at a high school in which he would manipulate noise during some test taking sessions, this would be an example of a
    a. quasi-experiment.
    b. field experiment.
    c. correlational study.
    d. observational study.

19. A research psychologist wants to see how different styles of leadership affect the amount of respect given to the assigned leader. In this example, style of leadership is the
    a. confederate.
    b. operational definition.
    c. dependent variable.
    d. independent variable.

20. Which of the following is NOT a way that researchers believe college students differ from the general population?
    a. College students come from more affluent families.
    b. College students are more intelligent.
    c. College students have more established self-concepts.
    d. College students have a smaller proportion of ethnic minorities.

True or False Questions

T F 1. A central theme in social psychology since the 1970s is the self.

T F 2. The scientific method is the main tool of social psychologists to sort valid conclusions from erroneous ones.

T F 3. Sociology is really no different than social psychology.

T F 4. Kurt Lewin once said, "There is nothing as practical as a good theory."

T F 5. Common wisdom is good enough for science.

T F 6. 80-90% of articles submitted for publication to the best journals are accepted.

T F 7. The independent variable is the variable that is manipulated in an experiment.

T F 8. Confederates are naïve participants who do not understand they are in a study.

T F 9. Experimental realism is more important than mundane realism in terms of determining external validity.

T F 10. Social psychologists are confident that their findings will generalize to people who live in all different cultures.

Short Essay Questions

1. What important contributions did Gordon Allport and Kurt Lewin make to the early development of social psychology?

2. Describe a study in which you use the following terms: independent variable, dependent variable, experimental realism, internal validity, and operational definitions.

3. Describe why science is self-correcting.

Suggested Readings

Adair, J. (2005). An introduction to the special issue: Social psychology around the world: Origins and subsequent development. *International Journal of Psychology, 40*(4), 209-212.

Eschman, A., James, J., Schneider, W., & Zuccolotto, A. (2005). PsychMate: Providing psychology majors the tools to do real experiments and learn empirical methods. *Behavior Research Methods, 37*(2), 301-311.

Pelham, B., & Blanton, H. (2006). *Conducting research in psychology: Measuring the weight of smoke* (3rd Ed.). Thomson-Wadsworth.

Sears, D. (1986). College sophomores in the laboratory: Influences of a narrow data base on social psychology's view of human nature. *Journal of Personality and Social Psychology, 51*(3), 515-530.

Wilson, T. (2005). The message is the method: Celebrating and exporting the experimental approach. *Psychological Inquiry, 16*(4), 185-193.

Answer Key

Section 1

Summary

1. Triplett, faster
2. Behaviorism, Freudian psycholanalysis

Section 2

Summary

1. affect, behavior, and cognition

Section 3

Understanding Terminology

1.	a	6.	d
2.	h	7.	g
3.	e	8.	i
4.	b	9.	c
5.	f	10.	j

Summary

1. social sciences, psychology

Section 4

Summary

1. Philosophy, social psychology, scientific method
2. applied research

Section 5

Understanding Terminology

1.	e	11.	k
2.	h	12.	o
3.	m	13.	g
4.	a	14.	d
5.	s	15.	l
6.	i	16.	f
7.	q	17.	j
8.	p	18.	c
9.	b	19.	t
10.	r	20.	n

Summary

1. Theories, hypothesis
2. chicken soup, number of white blood cells, experiment, randomly assigned, correlational approach

Section 6

Summary

1. replication, college students, generalizability

Chapter Test

Multiple Choice

1.	d	(p. 7)	11.	a	(p. 20)
2.	a	(p. 6)	12.	d	(p. 21)
3.	b	(p. 8)	13.	c	(p. 20)
4.	b	(p. 11)	14.	c	(p. 16)
5.	c	(p. 13)	15.	d	(p. 23)
6.	c	(p. 15)	16.	c	(p. 20)
7.	a	(p. 16)	17.	a	(p. 18)
8.	d	(p. 17)	18.	b	(p. 19)
9.	b	(p. 17)	19.	d	(p. 16)
10.	d	(p. 20)	20.	b	(p. 23)

True or False

1.	T	(p. 7)
2.	T	(p. 8)
3.	F	(p. 10)
4.	T	(p. 13)
5.	F	(p. 14)
6.	F	(p. 15)
7.	T	(p. 16)
8.	F	(p. 18)
9.	T	(p. 20)
10.	F	(p. 23)

Short Essay

1. What important contributions did Gordon Allport and Kurt Lewin make to the early development of social psychology?

- ❖ Gordon Allport – He observed that attitudes were the most important useful and concept in social psychology. Even today, attitudes continue to be a central area of study among social psychologists.
- ❖ Kurt Lewin – He is known for the impact of his insight that behavior is a function of the person and the situation. This idea still pervades much of the work in social psychology.

2. Describe a study in which you use the following terms: independent variable, dependent variable, experimental realism, internal validity, and operational definitions.

- ❖ Answers will vary, but must appropriately use each term. See definitions and uses of terms (pps. 14 – 21).

3. Describe why science is self-correcting.

- ❖ Science is self-correcting because new research is always building on past work, thus finding and correcting errors through replication. In other words, flawed conclusions will be discovered when new research is unable to replicate the finding.
- ❖ The body of knowledge is continuing to grow and is constantly self-correcting.

CHAPTER 2- CULTURE AND NATURE

CHAPTER REVIEW

Section 1: Explaining the Psyche

Snapshot

Humans have evolved through the process of natural selection to be cultural animals. It is the existence of culture that separates humans from the rest of the animal kingdom.

Learning Objectives

- Explain why understanding the purpose of the human psyche will help us understand human behavior.
- Describe how humans are impacted by both nature and culture.
- Define and explain natural selection, include two criteria of natural selection (staying alive and reproduction), how they work and their relative importance.
- Be able to describe the different reproductive strategies of men and women.
- Contrast the four different ways of understanding culture and its influence: culture as shared ideas, culture as system, culture as praxis, meaningful information shared in culture.
- Be able to describe how shared ideas, specifically laws, have their influence.
- Explain why the question of whether people are the same everywhere is an issue for social psychologists. Describe how people are the same and different across cultures.
- Contrast definition of humans as social animals and as cultural animals.

Understanding Terminology

Match the terms on the right to the definitions/examples on the left.

______ 1. Living to be able to reproduce.	a. natural selection
______ 2. Doing things in a way that is practical.	b. ideas
______ 3. A change in genetic make-up.	c. social animals
______ 4. For example, lightening, tigers, and heart valves.	d. sex
______ 5. Knowing what this is designed for will help us understand people.	e. nature
______ 6. Eating kim chi, speaking Korean, and co-sleeping.	f. praxis
______ 7. Humans are the only animals to be this.	g. evolution
______ 8. Desire to live, work, and connect with others.	h. psyche
______ 9. Term used to refer to sexuality.	i. gender
______ 10. "Survival of the fittest."	j. mutation
______ 11. Creating off-spring that survive to reproductive age.	k. survival
______ 12. Term used to describe differences between men and women.	l. cultural animals
______ 13. The theory of the process by which change occurs in nature.	m. culture
______ 14. Societal laws and rules are an example of this.	n. reproduction

Summary

Use the appropriate terms to complete each summary.

1. A debate has long raged about whether ____________________ or ____________________ is more important. Your text argues that it is not an "either-or" question, but instead that they have ____________________ one another.

2. Charles Darwin in his theory of ____________________, argued that animals evolved through the process of ____________________. In other words, ____________________ that are beneficial are likely to lead to greater success in ____________________.

3. We have evolved to be able to have __________________, in which to build our culture. Culture can also be thought of as including a shared way of doing things (e.g. culture as __________________). It is this ability to have, maintain, and share ideas that makes us __________________, not just __________________.

Section 2: The Individual and Society

Snapshot

Humans have evolved to have a brain capable of benefiting from culture. Culture benefits humans through the use of language, by building on past progress, by using division of labor, and by exchanging goods and services.

Learning Objectives

- ❖ Explain the social brain theory.
- ❖ Describe the main advantages of culture.
- ❖ Describe the various perspectives on the relationship of the individual and society.

Understanding Terminology

Match the terms on the right to the definitions/examples on the left.

_____ 1. Contributing to the culture in one's specialized way.	a. progress
_____ 2. Trusting one another in order to give money in exchange for goods/services.	b. division of labor
_____ 3. Building on the work, knowledge, and understanding of other humans.	c. network of trade and exchange

Summary

Use the appropriate terms to complete each summary.

1. According to the theory of evolution, the human brain evolved to allow us to have rich, complex __________________ lives. Research by Dunbar found that animals with bigger brains did not eat better foods or have larger territories, but they did have more complex __________________.

2. This larger brain has benefited humans by encouraging _________________. The main advantage of culture includes being able to share information and stories with _________________. Additionally, culture means that each person does not have to re-learn or re-invent what others have done, which allows _________________ to happen. Culture also allows people to specialize providing a _________________. Finally, we have evolved to be able to have _________________ relationships, allowing us to secure the things we need from others.

Section 3: Facts of Life

Snapshot

The influence of the interaction between culture and nature can be seen in the way people eat, have sex, and make tradeoffs. Humans are unique in the animal kingdom because <u>ideas</u> influence all of these domains.

Learning Objectives

- Explain how vegetarians show the impact of culture on human behavior.
- Explain how human sexual practices show the impact of culture on human behavior.
- Describe what is meant by the phrase "bad is stronger than good" and its relation to nature and culture.
- Describe the origin and subject matter of positive psychology.
- Define and explain tradeoffs.
- Contrast r-selected and k-selected reproductive strategies.
- Describe how nature and culture differ in tradeoffs involving time.
- Describe tradeoffs that appear in the political realm.

Summary

Use the appropriate terms to complete each summary.

1. Humans, unlike cows, mice, or iguanas, develop _________________ around food and sex. This occurs because humans have _________________ (what something means) about these things.

2. _________________ tends to be more powerful than _________________. In fact, to flourish, people need about _________________ positive emotions to each negative emotion experienced. Sometimes people must accept a cost or sacrifice a benefit in order to maximize other benefits. This is called a _________________.

Section 4: Important Features of Human Social Life

Snapshot

The human mind has two important systems: the automatic system and the conscious system. Both systems play a valuable role in human life. The conscious mind often puts the brakes on the automatic mind.

Learning Objectives

- Define and explain the duplex mind, including the differences between the two systems.
- Explain how the conscious and the automatic system work together.
- Describe why conscious override is important for culture.
- Describe the advantages and demands of living in culture.
- Explain the idea that inner processes serve interpersonal function.
- Describe how the automatic system and conscious system and impulses and culture are related.
- Explain the relationship of selfishness, natural selection, and culture.
- Describe how our perceptual systems are focused on correct perceptions (rather than detection) and on other human beings (rather than other species).
- Explain how putting people first is shown with food and in Asch's line judgment experiment.

Understanding Terminology

Match the terms on the right to the definitions/examples on the left.

______ 1. Fast, inflexible, and effortless.	a. duplex mind
______ 2. A modern version of Freud's conscious ego and unconscious.	b. conscious system
______ 3. Slow, flexible, and effortful.	c. automatic system

Summary

Use the appropriate terms to complete each summary.

1. The __________________ is made up of two systems. The __________________ mind is guided by intention and can make rule based calculations. The __________________ mind is good at making estimates and can do many things at once. The two systems often work together. The conscious system works like a(n) __________________, letting the automatic system know when something is wrong.

2. We have evolved to be able to relate well with other people. In other words, __________________ serve __________________. In order to live successfully in a complex world, our __________________ says go, but our __________________ says stop. This can be seen in the curbing of __________________ and in putting __________________ first.

Section 5: What Makes us Human? Putting the Cultural Animal in Perspective

Snapshot

Humans, like other animals, have many basic needs such as food, water, and shelter. However, humans are distinct from other animals because we have evolved to be cultural.

Learning Objectives

- ❖ Describe how being a cultural animal provides humans with an identity distinct from non-human animals.

Summary

Use the appropriate terms to complete each summary.

1. Human beings are unique because we have __________________. Culture does create problems (war, pollution), but the __________________ outweigh the __________________. Culture allows us to accumulate __________________ and pass it on!

CHAPTER TEST

Multiple Choice Questions

1. Rodrigo volunteers at the community center to teach younger children how to play baseball. Rodrigo's actions demonstrate how humans are
   a. cultural animals.
   b. social animals.
   c. surviving.
   d. shaped by nature.

2. "People shouldn't eat meat because animals have feelings" is an example of a(n) _______ .
   a. psyche
   b. idea
   c. culture
   d. system

3. The story of Brenda (the person born a boy, but raised a girl) highlights which of the following?
   a. Gender is completely shaped by society.
   b. There are limits to the power of socialization.
   c. It is much easier to raise a girl than a boy.
   d. All gender related behaviors are innate.

4. A recent movement called ___________ has begun to focus research on the good things in life.
   a. resilience
   b. human fulfillment
   c. focus on life
   d. positive psychology

5. The process of ________ chooses which traits will endure and which will disappear.
   a. culture
   b. assimiliation
   c. reproduction
   d. natural selection

6. When are people most likely to experience guilt?
   a. if they have exploited family or friends
   b. if they have exploited strangers
   c. if they have exploited the needy
   d. if they have exploited employers

7. Singing during the seventh inning stretch at a baseball game in America would be an example of
a. being a social animal.
b. an innate behavior.
c. culture.
d. a praxis.

8. In a restaurant, one person is the host, another is the server, a third prepares the salads, the fourth prepares the entrees, and the fifth prepares the pastries. Which advantage of the social brain does this best illustrate?
a. progress
b. language
c. exchange relationships
d. division of labor

9. If two animals had the same size brain, but animal A had a bigger body than animal B, which of the following statements would most likely be true?
a. Animal A is able to eat better/more food.
b. Animal B is able to eat better/more food.
c. Animal B belongs to a more complex social structure.
d. Animal A belongs to a more complex social structure.

10. Nathalie desires to study library and information science in order to begin to archive California's accomplishments for future generations. Which benefit of culture does this illustrate?
a. progress
b. division of labor
c. language
d. exchange relationships

11. The capacity to trust strangers and the tendency to feel guilty if you get more than you deserve fosters
a. progress.
b. division of labor.
c. language.
d. exchange relationships.

12. The fact that Van goes on diets, avoids food for religious reasons, and likes to eat in the company of others illustrates which important point?
a. Humans are not much different than other animals.
b. Ideas influence the ways we eat.
c. Eating and sex are both driven by nature.
d. Nature prevents humans from being too cultural.

13. Which of the following scenarios would have the most impact on Martina?
    a. Winning $50
    b. Losing $50
    c. No difference between A and B
    d. Psychologists would not have a prediction

14. Which of the following would greatly improve a person's happiness?
    a. Getting a new job that would lift the person from poverty
    b. Getting a new job that would double an already good income
    c. Going in for a routine check-up and finding out that you are extremely healthy

15. Maria Torres is a state senator. She is up for re-election. During her term she worked hard to come up with a compromise that would both protect the fishing industry and preserve the native fish population. If she wants to win re-election, she may
    a. promise to protect the fishing industry and the fish.
    b. acknowledge that she cannot do both.
    c. discuss the trade-offs.
    d. focus on just one of the sides.

16. The _____ mind is used to "figure it out." The ____ mind is used to "go with your gut feeling."
    a. duplex; single
    b. individualistic; collectivistic
    c. automatic; conscious
    d. conscious; automatic

17. Jaime is desperately trying to understand why Susan broke up with him. Which system of the mind is he most likely using?
    a. conscious
    b. automatic
    c. complex
    d. cultural

18. Which statement sums up the interplay between nature and culture?
    a. Nature and culture are like vinegar and oil.
    b. Nature and culture are two peas in a pod.
    c. Nature says go, Culture says stop.
    d. Nature says stop, Culture says go.

19. Which of the following is true about the human sensory system?
    a. Our sensory system is designed to help us perceive each other.
    b. Our sensory system is designed to help pick up stimuli from the natural environment.
    c. Our sensory system is designed to alert us to our surroundings.
    d. Our sensory system is designed to be better at detection than resolution.

20. The ________ is a broad term for the mind encompassing emotions, desires, and perceptions.
    a. social mind
    b. cultural mind
    c. psyche
    d. brain

True or False Questions

T F 1. Language makes the brain more powerful in that it allows the storage and retrieval of information.

T F 2. Charles Darwin coined the term "survival of the fittest" to explain natural selection.

T F 3. In Asch's famous study, the interesting result was that a large minority of participants relied more on their own experiences than other individuals.

T F 4. Women tend to prefer quality partners who are willing to commit.

T F 5. One of the basic goals of human life is to garner acceptance from others.

T F 6. Human brains only evolved to make us better at evading our enemies and finding more nutritional food.

T F 7. The requirements for social acceptance are stable across time and culture.

T F 8. Most Olympic athletes (in one study) were willing to give up future health for immediate success.

T F 9. Many species, including humans, are social animals.

T F 10. Negative/hurtful behaviors are more predictive of relationship outcomes than positive/warm behaviors.

Short Essay Questions

1. According to your text, in what ways are cultural animals different from social animals?

2. Describe the four benefits of culture that we are capable of because of our evolved brain.

3. What role do ideas play in making humans distinctively human?

Suggested Readings

Bargh, J., Gollwitzer, P., Lee-Chai, A., Barndollar, K., & Trotschel, R. (2001). The automated will: Nonconscious activation and pursuit of behavioral goals. *Journal of Personality and Social Psychology, 81*, 1014-1027.

Baumeister, R., Bratslavsky, E., Finkenauer, C., & Vohs, K. (2001). Bad is stronger than good. *Review of General Psychology, 5*, 323-370.

Eagly, A., & Wood, W. (1991). Explaining sex differences in social behavior: A meta-analytic perspective. *Personality and Social Psychology Bulletin*, *17*, 306-315.

Lieberman, M., Jarcho, J., & Obayashi, J. (2005). Attributional inference across cultures: Similar automatic attributions and different controlled corrections. *Personality and Social Psychology Bulletin, 31*, 889-901.

Schmitt, D., Shackelford, T., & Buss, D. (2001). Are men really more 'oriented' toward short-term mating than women? A critical review of theory and research. *Psychology, Evolution, & Gender, 3*, 211-239.

Answer Key

Section 1

Understanding Terminology

1.	k	8.	c
2.	f	9.	d
3.	j	10.	a
4.	e	11.	n
5.	h	12.	l
6.	m	13.	g
7.	l	14.	b

Summary

1. nature, culture, shaped
2. evolution, natural selection, mutations, reproduction
3. shared ideas, praxis, cultural animals, social animals

Section 2

Understanding Terminology

1. b
2. c
3. a

Summary

1. social, social structures
2. culture, one another, progress, division of labor, exchange

Section 3

Summary

1. cultural systems, ideas
2. bad, good, three, tradeoff

Section 4

Understanding Terminology

1. c
2. a
3. b

Summary

1. duplex mind, conscious, automatic, alarm
2. inner processes, interpersonal factors, nature, culture, selfishness, people

Section 5

Summary

1. culture, costs, benefits, knowledge

Chapter Test

Multiple Choice

1.	a	(p. 39)	11.	d	(p. 44)
2.	b	(p. 36)	12.	b	(p. 47)
3.	b	(p. 30)	13.	b	(p. 46)
4.	d	(p. 49)	14.	a	(p. 49)
5.	d	(p. 32)	15.	a	(p. 49)
6.	a	(p. 61)	16.	d	(p. 55)
7.	c	(p. 36)	17.	a	(p. 55)
8.	d	(p. 43)	18.	c	(p. 59)
9.	c	(p. 41)	19.	a	(p. 61)
10.	a	(p. 43)	20.	c	(p. 31)

True or False

1. T (p. 42)
2. F (p. 33)
3. F (p. 62)
4. T (p. 34)
5. T (p. 58)
6. F (p. 41)
7. F (p. 58)
8. T (p. 51)
9. T (p. 39)
10. T (p. 46)

Short Essay

1. According to your text, in what ways are cultural animals different from social animals?
   - Social Animals desire to be with others of the same species and prefer to live, work, and play together. Many species are quite social with one another.
   - Cultural Animals create and take part in culture. This includes using language and building on the work of others (progress). Cultural animals accumulate knowledge and desire to share and pass on knowledge. Only Humans are cultural animals.

2. Describe the four benefits of culture that we are capable of because of our evolved brain.
   - Language – allows the sharing of ideas, information, and stories.
   - Progress – means that each individual does not have to learn everything from scratch, but that we build upon the knowledge and inventions of those who came before us.
   - Division of Labor – it allows individuals to specialize. Without division of labor, each of us would have to collect our own food, sew our own clothes and build our own homes.
   - Exchanging goods and services – it is the system that allows us to take advantage of the division of labor. We can use our money or skills to trade for the things we need. This requires us to have some degree of trust in others and a sense of fairness.

3. What role do ideas play in making humans distinctively human?
   - Ideas are what separate humans from other species. Humans have ideas (mental representations that are abstract) that allow us to plan for the future, make progress, and think beyond our own needs. Without ideas, we would not have culture.

CHAPTER 3 – THE SELF

CHAPTER REVIEW

Section 1: What Is the Self?

Snapshot

The self is made up of three of three parts: self-knowledge, interpersonal self, and the agent self. Each of these serves a particular purpose. Our sense of self aids us in gaining social acceptance and in playing social roles. Self-awareness is important as it directs our attention inward and often helps us behave in ways that are culturally desired.

Learning Objectives

- Name and explain the three main parts of the self.
- Explain the origins of selfhood in terms of the individual and society.
- Describe the difference between self as impulse and self as institution and the impact of those on choices.
- Explain how selves are different in different cultures.
- Explain how the self helps us play social roles.
- Compare private and public self-awareness.
- Describe what happens when people compare themselves to standards.
- Explain the methods individuals use to escape self-awareness.
- Describe how eating binges allow for escaping the self.

Understanding Terminology

Match the terms on the right to the definitions/examples on the left.

______ 1. you tend to want to do what is best for the self if you have this construal	a. social roles
______ 2. a public performance	b. interpersonal self
______ 3. understanding how others see us	c. private self-awareness
______ 4. e.g., I am a female, I like elephants, and I am enrolled in social psychology	d. self as impulse
______ 5. thinking about how people see you	e. Self-regulation
______ 6. directing attention inward	f. public self-awareness
______ 7. ideals, norms, and expectations	g. agent self
______ 8. the part that says, "do this, decide this"	h. self-awareness
______ 9. employee, daughter, citizen	i. public self-consciousness
______ 10. sometimes referred to as the "true self"	j. independent self-construal
______ 11. you tend to want to do what is best for the group if you have this construal	k. self-knowledge
______ 12. the image I project of myself to others	l. interdependent self-construal
______ 13. controlling our own behaviors, thoughts, and feelings	m. standards
______ 14. being aware of our feelings, needs, and desires	n. self as institution

Summary

Use the appropriate terms to complete each summary.

1. The self consists of three parts: 1) ________________________ which consists of information about the self; 2) ________________________ which concerns self-presentation; 3 ________________________ which is involved in doing and making decisions.

2. It can be argued that the ________________________ is at the ________________________ between our physical bodies and the culture in which we reside. There are cultural and individual differences in what people consider the "true" self. Is it the ________________________ which consists of our inner thoughts and feelings or is ________________________ which is the way we are outwardly.

3. Research by Markus and Kitayama argues that people from different cultures have different self ________________________ . People from Asian cultures, in general, think of themselves more in terms of the groups to which they belong and are said to have ________________________ . People from Western cultures, in general, thinks of themselves more in terms of their unique characteristics and individuality and are said to have ________________________ .

4. People are sometimes ________________________ which means they are paying attention to themselves. Some research shows that people evaluate themselves against ________________________ when paying attention to themselves. This may result in people behaving ________________________ in some situations.

Section 2: Where Self-Knowledge Comes From

Snapshot

People come to know themselves by what others think of them (looking-glass self), by looking in (introspection), comparing themselves to others (social comparison), or by evaluating their own behavior (self-perception). People are motivated to have self-awareness because they desire to know the "truth" about themselves, they desire to improve themselves, and they desire to be consistent.

Learning Objectives

- Compare and contrast looking outside, looking inside, looking at others and looking at one's behavior (self-perception) as ways of gaining self-knowledge.
- Define phenomenal self (working self-concept).
- Describe why individuals would desire self-knowledge and which motive for self-knowledge tends to be strongest.
- Explain how the duplex mind is related to self-knowledge.
- Explain how self-handicapping allows individuals to maintain their own self-concept.

Understanding Terminology

Match the terms on the right to the definitions/examples on the left.

______	1. may cause us to dismiss criticism and inflate praise	a. social comparison
______	2. comparing oneself to others	b. generalized other
______	3. can inspire you to do better	c. self-perception theory
______	4. can make you feel good about yourself	d. consistency motive
______	5. I run because it feel good	e. intrinsic motivation
______	6. the sum total of other people	f. extrinsic motivation
______	7. I know myself by watching myself	g. looking-glass self
______	8. I run because it helps me lose weight	h. appraisal motive
______	9. only you can do this through privileged access	i. phenomenal self
______	10. extrinsic rewards for what was intrinsically rewarding causes this	j. self-enhancement motive
______	11. the desire to know one's "true" self	k. overjustification effect
______	12. we know who we are through the eyes of others	l. introspection
______	13. self-verification motive	m. upward social comparison
______	14. the aspect of yourself that you are currently thinking about	n. downward social comparison
______	15. automatic response of "good = me; bad = not me"	o. self-handicapping
______	16. preparing an excuse in advance for potential failure.	p.automatic egotism

Summary

Use the appropriate terms to complete each summary.

1. Cooley used the term ______________________ to describe how we come to know ourselves by the way other people view us. Sometimes it is a specific other person, but more often it the ______________________, or the combination of all other people.

2. Except for young children, most people understand that they have ______________________ to themselves and use ______________________ to understand who they are. However, research has shown that we often are not very good at looking inside and understanding ourselves. Another way to know ourselves is by comparing ourselves to other people. Sometimes we make ______________________ in order to improve our selves and learn how to do things better. Other times we make ______________________ in order to make ourselves feel better.

3. People may infer their feelings and attitudes by looking to their own ______________________. This is called ______________________. Research has found that when people are rewarded for what they previously enjoyed doing without external reward, their intrinsic motivation for the activity declines and the ______________________ effect occurs.

Section 3: Self and Information Processing

Snapshot

Individuals tend to remember things and like things better if they are associated with the self. The self-reference effect and the endowment effect both illustrate our self favoring bias. The self-concept is very stable and often resistant to change, unless our social worlds change.

Learning Objectives

- Describe the self-reference effect and how it works.
- Explain whether or not the self-concept can change and the effect that has on the stories people tell about the self.

Summary

Use the appropriate terms to complete each summary.

1. The ____________________ effect states that information about the self is processed more deeply and remembered better than other information. Even things that are associated with the self become more ____________________, this is called the ____________________ .

2. If people want to change, they should enlist their family and friends to support the change. For example, if you want to start exercising, you want your family and friends to ____________________ your change. However, once a person has changed, they will often ____________________ the story of how they use to be.

Section 4: Self-Esteem, Self-Deception, and Positive Illusions

Snapshot

Self-esteem is how favorably or unfavorably a person evaluates him or herself. People with high self-esteem tend to see the world in a biased manner consisting of positive illusions while people with low self-esteem are more realistic in the way they view the world. High self-esteem is not universally a good thing and is associated with some negatives such as narcissism, prejudice and aggression.

Learning Objectives

- Define self-esteem and the characteristics of those high and low in self-esteem
- Explain how illusions about the self might be good for people.
- Identify the self-deception strategies that individuals use.
- Describe how the theme of inner structures serving interpersonal processes is illustrated in our desire to protect and increase our self-esteem.
- Describe the drawbacks of high self-esteem, including how narcissism fits into the picture.
- Describe the impact of different ways of pursuing self-esteem.

Understanding Terminology

Match the terms on the right to the definitions/examples on the left.

______ 1. the degree to which a person feels positively about themselves	a. self-deception strategies
______ 2. measures how socially acceptable you are in certain roles.	b. self-serving bias
______ 3. a way to believe what is objectively untrue	c. sociometer
______ 4. a desire to maintain self-esteem	d. self-esteem
______ 5. being in love with own self	e. self-protection
______ 6. I earned the A, but the F was unfair	f. narcissism

Summary

Use the appropriate terms to complete each summary.

1. People with ____________________ tend to evaluate themselves very favorably. People with ____________________ evaluate themselves less positively and may show ____________________ which means they may have uncertain or conflicted ideas about themselves.

2. Self views are often inaccurate, especially among people who are not ____________________ . Non-depressed individuals tend to be characterized by three different positive illusions. 1) They ____________________ their good qualities. 2) They overestimate their ____________________ over events. 3) They are unrealistically ____________________ .

3. In order to maintain positive illusions, people fool themselves with ____________________ . The ____________________ enables people to interpret events in a way that takes credit for positive things and denies blame for negative things. People are also more ____________________ of critical feedback than positive feedback.

4. Research has shown that self-esteem is not necessarily a good thing as it has been associated with ____________________, or self love. Additionally, people who think positively of themselves also tend to think positively of their group which leads to ____________________ and ____________________ .

Section 5: Self Presentation

Snapshot

Humans are often interested in controlling their self-presentation. People want others to think good things about them and often will alter their behavior or engage in risky behavior to control self-presentation. Having a good self-presentation is a way to garner social acceptance, something everyone wants.

Learning Objectives

❖ Define self-presentation and identify when people engage in self-presentation. Explain when people are likely to focus on making a good impression on their audience and why they might occasionally go against that (in claiming identity and in modesty).

Summary

Use the appropriate terms to complete each summary.

1. ______________________ is defined as any behavior that seeks to convey an image or information about the self to others. Self-presentation concerns is why we sometimes behave differently in ______________________ compared to in ______________________ . Self-presentation seems most relevant when making ______________________ , but less important in well-established relationships.

CHAPTER TEST

Multiple Choice Questions

1. If self-aware people notice an unpleasant discrepancy between themselves and some standard, they are likely to attempt to do one of two things. What are these two strategies?
   a. change or escape
   b. re-evaluate or change
   c. change standards or override standards
   d. self-deceive or introspect

2. On the first day of the class, your professor may dress particularly professional, show up to class 15 minutes early, and stand very straight. You are seeing the
   a. interdependent self.
   b. self as impulse.
   c. self as institution.
   d. independent self.

3. I am a daughter; I am a member of the volleyball team; I am a best friend. According to these descriptors, it would be reasonable to conclude that I have a(n)
   a. independent self-construal.
   b. interdependent self-construal.
   c. private self-awareness.
   d. public self-awareness.

4. Which of the following is TRUE about self-awareness?
   a. Self-awareness makes people act more consistent with their attitudes.
   b. Self-awareness always results in more socially acceptable behavior.
   c. Self-awareness tends to go up when drinking alcohol.
   d. All of the above are TRUE.

5. Suzy has always enjoyed playing with markers. Her parents decide that playing with markers has a lot of benefits for Suzy so they decide give her candy each time she plays with markers. A few months later, her parents decide to no longer give her candy. What is likely to happen?
   a. Suzy stops playing with the markers.
   b. Suzy continues to play with the markers because she really like to.
   c. Suzy plays with the markers even more than before.

6. Johnny is an average basketball player. If he wants to improve his game, he is likely to make
   a. downward social comparisons.
   b. upward social comparisons.
   c. comparisons to the generalized other.
   d. equal social comparisons.

7. Which of the following is a component of the looking-glass self?
   a. You imagine how you appear to others.
   b. You imagine how others will judge you.
   c. You develop an emotion response to how you think others will judge you.
   d. All of the above are components of the looking-glass self.

8. The night before the GRE exam, Hannah decides to go out with friends drinking. If she does badly, she can say it was because of her hangover; if she does well, it makes it all that much more impressive. What is this called?
   a. consistency motive
   b. phenomenal self
   c. self-handicapping
   d. automatic egotism

9. All other things being equal, what city is Frida likely to choose to live?
   a. Anchorage
   b. Fresno
   c. San Diego
   d. Madison

10. You are at a party and you hear someone talking about movies. One of the movies mentioned is your favorite movie. The fact that you are more likely to remember that this movie was mentioned than the others is called the
a. endowment effect.
b. egotism effect.
c. spotlight effect.
d. self-reference effect.

11. Often, after going through a program for self-improvement, even if no improvement occurs, people think they have improved. Why?
a. People revise their recollection of the past to indicate improvement.
b. People always think they are improving.
c. People fall victim to the self-reference effect.
d. People are optimistic.

12. If I buy old baseball cards for $1 each and then my little brother asks if he can buy them from me, the endowment effect would suggest which of the following scenarios?
a. I refuse to sell them, because they have become part of my self-concept.
b. I sell them for $1 each because my brother is family.
c. I say I will sell them for $2 each because I think they are worth that.
d. I say I will sell them for $2 each because I am motivated by profit.

13. When I score a goal in a soccer game it is because I am a talented player, but when I fail to score a goal in the game it is because the field was slippery. This is an example of
a. the self-serving bias.
b. an ego motive.
c. the self-reference effect.
d. self-efficacy.

14. A young man who fell in love with his own reflection would be said to have
a. high self-esteem.
b. narcissism.
c. positive illusions.
d. unrealistic beliefs.

15. People with low self-esteem may show a pattern called "self-concept confusion." Which of the following would NOT fit this pattern?
a. They may be uncertain about how to answer questions about themselves.
b. They may give contradictory answers about themselves.
c. They may describe themselves differently on different days.
d. They may insist that they are better than they really are.

16. The fact that college students are more likely to wear their school colors on the day after their team won is a example of
a. blasting.
b. basking in reflected glory.
c. self-serving bias.
d. positive illusions.

17. What concern does the desire to make good first impressions illustrate?
a. self-esteem
b. self-awareness
c. automatic egotism
d. self-presentation

18. Which phrase is NOT indicative of self-presentation?
a. "No one would diet on a deserted island."
b. "To thy own self be true."
c. "It is more important to look good than feel good!"

19. Which of the following is true about the way college students rated themselves on a variety of characteristics?
a. 70% of students thought they were better than average in leadership.
b. 50% of students thought they were below average in driving ability.
c. 15% of students thought they were below average in leadership.
d. 75% of students thought they were above average in ability to get along with others.

20. What is the sociometer theory of self-esteem?
a. Self-esteem is derived from our inner strengths and virtues.
b. Self-esteem is important for our success in the world.
c. Self-esteem is derived through social comparison.
d. Self-esteem is important for social acceptance.

True or False Questions

T F 1. Women with eating disorders may lose self-awareness during binge eating.

T F 2. Humans are flexible and can take on new and changing social roles.

T F 3. The overjustification effect predicts that the more a professional athlete gets paid the more they will enjoy the game.

T F 4. Once people have opinions about themselves, they are motivated to maintain those beliefs.

T F 5. One's social world is a powerful source of self-concept stability.

T F 6. It was easier to brainwash American soldiers if they were kept in groups with other American soldiers.

T F 7. People with low self-esteem are more likely to risk failure to pursue an opportunity.

T F 8. Research has shown that high self-esteem leads to better grades in school.

T F 9. People are usually more concerned with their own self-esteem than their self-presentation.

T F 10. People can use self-presentation to claim an identity.

Short Essay Questions

1. How do people with high self-esteem differ from people with low self-esteem?

2. What are three positive illusions that characterize many people's thought processes?

3. What is self-presentation and why do people engage in it?

Suggested Readings

Bushman, B., & Baumeister, R. (2002). Does self-love or self-hate lead to violence?. *Journal of Research in Personality*, *36*(6), 543-545.

Hewitt, P. L., Flett, G. L., & Sherry, S. B. (2003). The interpersonal expression of perfection: Perfectionistic self-presentation and psychological distress. *Journal of Personality and Social Psychology*, *84*(6), 1303-1325.

Leary, M. (2004). The Self We Know and the Self We Show: Self-esteem, Self-presentation, and the Maintenance of Interpersonal Relationships. *Emotion and motivation* (pp. 204-224). Blackwell Publishing.

Markus, H., & Kitayama, S. (1991). Culture and the self: Implications for cognition, emotion, and motivation. *Psychological Review*, *98*(2), 224-253.

Taylor, S., & Brown, J. (1988). Illusion and well-being: A social psychological perspective on mental health. *Psychological Bulletin*, *103*(2), 193-210.

Answer Key

Section 1

Understanding Terminology

1.	j	8.	e
2.	n	9.	a
3.	f	10.	d
4.	k	11.	l
5.	i	12.	b
6.	c	13.	g
7.	m	14.	h

Summary

1. self-knowledge, interpersonal self, agent self
2. self, interface, self as impulse, self as institution
3. construals, interdependent self-construal, independent self-construal
4. self-aware, standards, better

Section 2

Understanding Terminology

1. j
2. a
3. m
4. n
5. e
6. b
7. c
8. f
9. l
10. k
11. h
12. g
13. d
14. i
15. p
16. o

Summary

1. looking-glass self, generalized other
2. privileged access, introspection, upward social comparison, downward social comparison
3. behavior, self-perception theory, overjustification

Section 3

Summary

1. self-reference, valuable, endowment effect
2. support, revise

Section 4

Understanding Terminology

1. d
2. c
3. a
4. e
5. f
6. b

Summary

1. high self-esteem, low self-esteem, self-concept confusion
2. depressed, overestimate, perceived control, optimistic
3. self-deception strategies, self-serving bias, skeptical
4. narcissism, prejudice, discrimination

Section 5

Summary

1. self-presentation, public, private, first impressions

Chapter Test

Multiple Choice

1.	a	(p. 76)	11.	a	(p. 94)
2.	c	(p. 73)	12.	a	(p. 91)
3.	b	(p. 73)	13.	a	(p. 99)
4.	a	(p. 77)	14.	b	(p. 103)
5.	a	(p. 83)	15.	d	(p. 95)
6.	b	(p. 83)	16.	b	(p. 97)
7.	d	(p. 80)	17.	d	(p. 106)
8.	c	(p. 89)	18.	b	(p. 106)
9.	b	(p. 91)	19.	a	(p. 96)
10.	d	(p. 90)	20.	d	(p. 102)

True or False

1.	T	(p. 79)
2.	T	(p. 75)
3.	F	(p. 84)
4.	T	(p. 87)
5.	T	(p. 92)
6.	F	(p. 93)
7.	F	(p. 96)
8.	F	(p. 100)
9.	F	(p. 105)
10.	T	(p. 108)

Short Essay

1. How do people with high self-esteem differ from people with low self-esteem?

- Individuals with high self-esteem hold favorable views of themselves. They may consider themselves good, likable, moral people.
- People with low self-esteem, unlike some people think, do not necessarily hold negative views of themselves, instead they hold more neutral views. Like people with high self-esteem people with low self-esteem have goals and do not want to fail. They may be less confident in their abilities. People with low self-esteem may show self-concept confusion and focus on self-protection.

2. What are three positive illusions that characterize many people's thought processes?

- People overestimate their good qualities
- People overestimate their perceived control over events
- People are unrealistically optimistic

3. What is self-presentation and why do people engage in it?

- Self-presentation is behavior that is intended to portray a certain image to other people. This is a broad idea that encompasses all behaviors that we engage in either consciously or unconsciously to give others a certain idea about ourselves.
- People engage in self-presentation to make a good impression (e.g. have others like us) and sometimes to claim a particular identity.

CHAPTER 4 – BEHAVIOR CONTROL: THE SELF IN ACTION

CHAPTER REVIEW

Section 1: What You Do, and What It Means

Snapshot

Humans are unique in that they use ideas and meanings to shape their lives and interpersonal functions. Humans are also unique in that they form both short and long-term goals and develop plans to achieve those goals.

Learning Objectives

- Describe how levels of meaning influence action and how these might change.
- Contrast entity theorists and incremental theorists.
- Explain how individuals set and pursue goals.
- Describe the place of planning in reaching a goal, as well as the mistakes one might make in planning.

Understanding Terminology

Match the terms on the right to the definitions/examples on the left.

______ 1. Giving up after past failure.	a. goal
______ 2. It will take me 6 hours to write my paper (it actually took 9).	b. Zeigarnik effect
______ 3. Dislike of criticism and negative feedback.	c. learned helplessness
______ 4. Mental interruptions following a disruption of a goal.	d. entity theorists
______ 5. Work hard to improve and enjoys challenging tasks.	e. planning fallacy
______ 6. The important link between our values and our actions.	f. incremental theorists

Summary

Use the appropriate terms to complete each summary.

1. Human behavior is influenced by more than reward and __________________ . Meanings and __________________ play an important role in human behavior. Research has shown that different levels of meanings exist and that people are more persuadable when their attention is focused on __________________ levels of meaning.

2. There are two important steps to pursuing goals. The first step includes __________________ . Next, an individual must __________________ the goal. Research shows that individuals are more __________________ when setting goals and more __________________ when pursuing goals. In order to reach a distant goal, people must also have a __________________ of goals.

3. Planning is an important aspect of reaching goals. People often fall victim to the __________________ , or the belief that their project will proceed as planned, even if others will not.

Section 2: Freedom and Choice

Snapshot

Although the question of free will has been debated for centuries, there is little doubt that people perceive that they have choices. Sometimes we make choices because of internal pressure (private desires, joys, and goals) or external pressures (pressure from others). Many things influence what we choose including risk aversion, temporal discounting, the certainty effect, and the desire to keep our options open.

Learning Objectives

- Explain the role of freedom in human action, including self-determination theory and the panic button effect.
- Describe the two steps of choosing.
- Explain the five major patterns guiding people's choices (risk aversion, temporal discounting, certainty effect, keeping options open, and reactance).
- Describe the relative importance to people of avoiding losses versus pursuing goals.
- Explain how error management theory helps us understand differences between men and women in interpreting friendly gestures/sexual invitations.

Understanding Terminology

Match the terms on the right to the definitions/examples on the left.

______ 1. If a person feels they can escape a stressful situation, the situation holds less power.	a. certainty effect
______ 2. Gives more weight to things that are certain compared to the unknowns.	b. omission bias
______ 3. "Doing something by doing nothing."	c. self-determination theory
______ 4. People need to feel that they make some of their own decisions based on their internal states.	d. temporal discounting
______ 5. People are more likely to choose to keep things the same, even if change may hold benefits.	e. reactance theory
______ 6. Men do not want to miss out on opportunities and women do not want to miss a better alternative.	f. status quo bias
______ 7. The chance of losing $10 is more powerful than the chance of winning $10.	g. error management theory
______ 8. Theorizes that a person will act to restore freedom when it is threatened.	h. panic button effect
______ 9. Focus more on current rewards than future rewards.	i. risk aversion

Summary

Use the appropriate terms to complete each summary.

1. People have a need to be ___________________ , which is a central tenet of self-determination theory. People are generally more satisfied with, interested in, and excited about actions that they take because of ___________________ motivation.

2. The choices we make are influenced by a number of biases and errors. For example, people are more motivated to avoid potential ___________________ than go after possible gains. This is called ___________________ . People also show the ___________________ bias when they prefer to keep things as they are, even if a change may be an improvement. The ___________________ bias is similar in that people often "make decisions" by doing nothing at all.

Section 3: Self-Regulation

Snapshot

Self-regulation is synonymous with self-control and is about our ability to allow one's social conscience to prevail over our selfish impulses. Self-regulation involves standards, monitoring, and strength.

Learning Objectives

- ❖ Describe self-regulation and the three major components of self-regulation.
- ❖ Explain the importance of self-regulation to dieting.

Understanding Terminology

Match the terms on the right to the definitions/examples on the left.

_____ 1. An example would be keeping a diary of calories consumed.	a. Monitoring
_____ 2. Using willpower to exert self-control.	b. TOTE
_____ 3. Controlling one's impulses to act in accord with social standards.	c. self-regulation
_____ 4. The feedback loop that helps us self-regulate.	d. capacity for change

Summary

Use the appropriate terms to complete each summary.

1. ___________________ allows us to adapt to social demands. Self regulation consists of three important components: ___________________ , ___________________, and ___________________ . Research has shown that ___________________ is like a muscle and can be exhausted after use, but grow stronger with exercise.

Section 4: Irrationality and Self-Destruction

Snapshot

People sometimes engage in self-defeating behavior which may bring pain, failure, and misfortune. However, people do not engage in this behavior to encounter this negative outcomes, but instead are either making tradeoffs or basing their decisions on faulty knowledge or flawed strategies.

Learning Objectives

- Describe how self-defeating behavior is a paradox.
- Describe the two main reasons for self-defeating behavior.
- Define the capacity to delay gratification and what research studies have revealed about it.
- Explain the tradeoff involved in a decision to commit suicide.
- Describe how expectations, self-awareness, and meaning help us understand suicide.

Summary

Use the appropriate terms to complete each summary.

1. Individuals engage in self-defeating behaviors because negative outcomes are linked with positive outcomes, thus they are making ___________________. Other times, people base decisions on ___________________ or flawed strategies.

2. Research has shown that individuals that can ___________________ are often likely to find greater success in the long-term.

3. ___________________ is a behavior that is virtually unknown among non-human animals. Although severe, it is likely seen as a ___________________, in which immediate relief is sacrificed for future opportunities.

CHAPTER TEST

Multiple Choice Questions

1. In a study, researchers had some college students imagine themselves studying hard for an exam and doing well and other students just keep track of their studying. What did the researchers find?
a. Students who imagined studying did poorer on the exam because they felt less of a need to study after the imagination exercise.
b. Students who imagined studying did better on the exam and actually did study longer and harder.
c. It was only imagining doing better on the exam that seemed to impact actual performance.
d. There were no differences: imagining does not help students.

2. If a student is experiencing anxiety over a test, they may want to try to
a. focus on the higher levels of meaning.
b. remember the distal goal.
c. avoid meaning altogether.
d. focus on the lower levels of meaning.

3. I am a(n) ___ theorist if I think that with hard work, I can improve my soccer skills.
a. behavioral
b. evolutionary
c. entity
d. incremental

4. ___ tend to have goals that emphasize fulfillment, safety, and flexibility compared to ___ .
a. Women, men
b. Men, women
c. Older people, younger people
d. Younger people, older people

5. Plans have two major drawbacks. One is that they can be discouraging if too rigid or detailed. What is the other major drawback?
a. Goals tend to distract people from more important tasks.
b. Goals tend to be self-serving and not focus on other people.
c. Goals may be poorly chosen and thus not beneficial.
d. Goals tend to be overly optimistic.

6. Among humans, freedom is marked by all of the following except which one?
   a. behavioral flexibility
   b. total rationality
   c. controlled processes
   d. self-regulation

7. Ryan and Chad both have set a goal to run a mile under 6 minutes. Ryan is motivated by the love of running and internal desire to improve. Chad is motivated by a promise of $100 from his dad if he accomplishes the goal. Both Ryan and Chad reach their goal. Which scenario is most likely true?
   a. Ryan feels happier than Chad.
   b. Chad feels happier than Ryan.
   c. Both Ryan and Chad are equally happy about meeting their goal.
   d. Both Ryan and Chad are looking for the next challenge.

8. Sofia is trying to decide if she wants to go back to school. If she decides to go to school, she needs to fill out an application and take a test. If she decides not to go to school, she does not need to do anything. In the end, she decides to not return to school. This may be an example of
   a. risk aversion.
   b. temporal discounting.
   c. the certainty effect.
   d. the omission bias.

9. If person is offered $100 or a 1 in 3 chance of $500, she may choose the $100 because of the
   a. risk aversion.
   b. temporal discounting.
   c. the certainty effect.
   d. the omission bias.

10. Cindy's parents tell her that she cannot see her boyfriend Sean any more because they want her to date "nicer boys." She is likely to experience
    a. reactance.
    b. risk aversion.
    c. the panic button effect.
    d. the certainty effect.

11. What does the acronym TOTE stand for?
    a. Test, Operate, Target, Exit
    b. Test, Operate, Test, Evaluate
    c. Test, Operate, Test, Exit
    d. Target, Operate, Test, Evaluate

12. Which of the following is not one of the main components of self-regulation?
a. monitoring
b. choice
c. standards
d. strength

13. Wally is very hungry, but decides to use his willpower and not eat the cookies in order to wait for a healthy meal. Which of the following most closely resembles the understanding of willpower?
a. Wally's willpower is likely to be depleted in the short-term but strengthened in the long-term.
b. Wally's willpower is likely strengthened in the short-term but weaker for the future.
c. Willpower is not effected by recent use.
d. Each time willpower is used, it is immediately strengthened.

14. Which of the following refers to a concept that captures our cultures rules?
a. monitoring
b. ideas
c. capacity for change
d. standards

15. Laura often engages in what appears to be "stupid" behavior. She may do this because of
a. faulty knowledge.
b. tradeoffs.
c. a and b.
d. none of the above.

16. Which of the following strategies did children use to help them delay gratification?
a. focused on self-awareness
b. do something so that the reward wasn't in view
c. made risk averse decisions
d. set goals on how long to wait

17. An example of a tradeoff that sometimes results in self-defeating behavior is
a. self-serving bias.
b. status-quo bias.
c. planning fallacy.
d. self-handicapping.

18. As our culture progresses, there seems to be
    a. more and more choices.
    b. fewer choices.
    c. similar number of choices.

19. The _____ may be important for keeping track of goals and initiating behavior, but the_____ may be important when a goal is blocked and flexibility is needed.
    a. automatic system, conscious system
    b. conscious system, automatic system
    c. internal motivational system, external motivational system
    d. external motivational system, internal motivations system

20. If you are a salesperson trying to sell a computer system to a customer, you would be well served if you could focus the customer's attention on
    a. high levels of meaning.
    b. low levels of meaning.
    c. their long-term goals.
    d. their standards.

True or False Questions

T F 1. When emotions are positive, people like to move to higher levels of meaning.

T F 2. Most people experience the Zeigarnik effect after accomplishing a long-held goal.

T F 3. Simply having an escape from a stressful situation may reduce the negative outcomes associated with the stress, even if the escape is never used.

T F 4. The two steps of making choices are: first focusing on your own desires and likes and then evaluating each possible choice.

T F 5. Error management theory relies on the fact that throughout our history, women have had a very difficult time getting pregnant.

T F 6. People who excel at self-regulation are more likely to succeed in many realms.

T F 7. Dieters find more success when they do not closely monitor their food intake.

T F 8. Research has found that binge eating among dieters is a result of a failure of self-monitoring.

T F 9. Most studies have found that suicidal people are full of anxiety, regret, and guilt.

T F 10. Self-defeating behavior is paradoxical.

Short Essay Questions

1. The behavior of writing a lover a poem may have multiple levels of meaning. Describe several different levels of meaning.

2. How is reactance associated with freedom?

3. What are the three components of self-regulation? Describe the three components.

Suggested Readings

Fiske, S. (1992). Thinking is for doing: Portraits of social cognition from Daguerreotype to laserphoto. *Journal of Personality and Social Psychology*, *63*(6), 877-889.

Kruger, J., & Evans, M. (2004). If you don't want to be late, enumerate: Unpacking reduces the planning fallacy. *Journal of Experimental Social Psychology*, *40*(5), 586-598.

Lester, D., Wood, P., Williams, C., & Haines, J. (2004). Motives for suicide-A study of Australian suicide notes. *Crisis: The Journal of Crisis Intervention and Suicide Prevention*, *25*(1), 33-34.

Vartanian, L., Herman, C., & Polivy, J. (2006). Does regulatory focus play a role in dietary restraint? *Eating Behaviors*, *7*(4), 333-341.

Weber, B., & Chapman, G. (2005). The combined effects of risk and time on choice: Does uncertainty eliminate the immediacy effect? Does delay eliminate the certainty effect? *Organizational Behavior and Human Decision Processes*, *96*(2), 104-118.

Wegner, D., Vallacher, R., & Dizadji, D. (1989). Do alcoholics know what they're doing? Identifications of the act of drinking. *Basic and Applied Social Psychology*, *10*(3), 197-210.

Answer Key

Section 1

Understanding Terminology

1. c
2. e
3. d
4. b
5. f
6. a

Summary

1. punishment, ideas, low
2. setting goals, pursue, realistic, optimistic, hierarchy
3. planning fallacy

Section 2

Understanding Terminology

1. h
2. a
3. b
4. c
5. f
6. g
7. i
8. e
9. d

Summary

1. autonomous, intrinsic
2. loss, risk aversion, status quo, omission

Section 3

Understanding Terminology

1. a
2. d
3. c
4. b

Summary

1. self-regulation, standards, monitoring, strength, willpower

Section 4

Summary

1. tradeoffs, faulty knowledge
2. delay gratification
3. suicide, tradeoff

Chapter Test

Multiple Choice

1.	b	(p. 118)	11.	c	(p. 133)
2.	c	(p. 118)	12.	b	(p. 133)
3.	d	(p. 120)	13.	a	(p. 134)
4.	a	(p. 121)	14.	d	(p. 133)
5.	d	(p. 124)	15.	c	(p. 137)
6.	b	(p. 126)	16.	b	(p. 138)
7.	a	(p. 127)	17.	d	(p. 137)
8.	d	(p. 130)	18.	a	(p. 128)
9.	c	(p. 129)	19.	a	(p. 123)
10.	a	(p. 131)	20.	b	(p. 118)

True or False

1. T (p. 118)
2. F (p. 122)
3. T (p. 127)
4. F (p. 128)
5. F (p. 130)
6. T (p. 132)
7. F (p. 133)
8. T (p. 134)
9. F (p. 139)
10. T (p. 136)

Short Essay

1. The behavior of writing a lover a poem may have multiple levels of meaning. Describe several different levels of meaning.

- Low level – moving hand to form letters
- Mid level – creating sentences
- High level – conveying message of love and commitment

2. How is reactance associated with freedom?

- When individuals feel their freedom or choice is being usurped by others, they may experience three consequences: 1) the forbidden choice becomes even more appealing, 2) work to assert or reclaim freedom or choice, and 3) feel or act aggressively toward the person who restricted freedom.

3. What are the three components of self-regulation? Describe the three components.

- Standards – the ideas or goals of what you should or could be (often culturally defined).
- Monitoring – tracking the behavior that you want to regulate.
- Strength – an understanding that it takes willpower (specific focus or energy) to control behavior. This strength can be depleted after being used.

CHAPTER 5 – SOCIAL COGNITION

CHAPTER REVIEW

Section 1: What Is Social Cognition?

Snapshot

Humans spend a lot of time thinking about other people. People often are cognitive misers relying on effortless automatic thinking, but sometimes engage in more controlled intentional thought. To aid in automatic thinking, people have knowledge structures that consist of schemas and scripts.

Learning Objectives

- Define social cognition.
- Describe how thinking about people is different.
- Define cognitive miser and how being cognitive misers affects people's thinking.
- Provide the three major goals of thinking
- Describe how the Stroop test illustrates the difference between automatic and controlled thinking.
- Explain knowledge structures and their relation with schemas, scripts, priming, and framing.
- Describe how the automatic and controlled processes work in thought suppression.
- Explain counterregulation and how it helps explain dieters' behavior.

Understanding Terminology

Match the terms on the right to the definitions/examples on the left.

_____ 1. The finding that it is difficult to override an automatic tendency.	a. knowledge structures
_____ 2. Being stingy with thinking.	b. framing
_____ 3. Information stored in memory that if activated can run on auto-pilot.	c. social cognition
_____ 4. Knowledge structures that direct our behavior in certain situations.	d. stroop test
_____ 5. When a stimulus activates a knowledge structure.	e. stroop effect
_____ 6. "What the heck" thinking.	f. scripts
_____ 7. A classic test to demonstrate the challenge of effortful control.	g. counterregulation
_____ 8. Often, a message can be presented in positive terms or negative terms.	h. priming
_____ 9. Thinking by people about people.	i. schemas
_____ 10. Knowledge structures about a particular concept.	j. cognitive miser

Summary

Use the appropriate terms to complete each summary.

1. ____________________ is studying how people think about other people and their relationships with them. The mind has ____________________ to form relationships with others and thus its primary job is to think about other people.

2. There are three goals of thinking according to the text. The first goal is to find the ____________________. The second goal is to find the ____________________. And the final goal is to reach a ____________________ very quickly. The third goal relies most heavily on ____________________ thinking while the first two goals may require more ____________________ thinking.

3. Information is stored in memory as ____________________. ____________________ are a specific type of knowledge structure that is about how to perform some behavior, while a ____________________ is a knowledge structure that contains information about some particular concept.

Section 2: Attributions: Why Did That Happen?

Snapshot

Individuals quite often try to explain their own or other people's behavior. Interestingly, the explanations we give often depend upon whose behavior we are explaining. In explaining our own behavior, we tend to make the self-serving bias, but when explaining other people's behavior, we tend to make the fundamental attribution error. The explanations we make can determine how we react toward other people and our own future behavior.

Learning Objectives

- ❖ Define attribution and the early research on the aspects of attribution.
- ❖ Explain the actor/observer bias, the fundamental attribution error, and the ultimate attribution error.
- ❖ Work with Harold Kelly's attribution cube.

Understanding Terminology

Match the terms on the right to the definitions/examples on the left.

______ 1. Does this person behave this way in other situations?	a. covariation principle
______ 2. I did it because of the situation; you did it because you are grouchy.	b. self-serving bias
______ 3. Does this person always behave this way in this situation?	c. fundamental attribution error
______ 4. To be the cause, it must be present when it occurs and otherwise absent.	d. consensus
______ 5. I got an A because I am smart, the F was because the test was unfair.	e. ultimate attribution error
______ 6. Do other people behave this way in the same situation?	f. attribution cube
______ 7. Applying the fundamental attribution to an entire group of people.	g. attributions
______ 8. Overusing internal attributions and under-using external attributions.	h. distinctiveness
______ 9. Explaining our own and other people's behavior.	i. consistency
______ 10. Uses consensus, consistency, and distinctiveness information in attributions.	j. actor/observer bias

Summary

Use the appropriate terms to complete each summary.

1. Taking credit for successes and denying blame for failure is called the __________________. However, when judging other people's behavior we tend to overestimate __________________ causes and underestimate __________________ causes. This is called the __________________

2. Theorist Harold Kelley proposed that individuals answer a number of questions to ascertain when the behavior typically occurs and does not occur. This idea is called the __________________ . He used three types of information to conclude covariation. These included __________________, __________________, and __________________ .

Section 3: Heuristics: Mental Shortcuts

Snapshot

In order to save mental energy, people often take predictable shortcuts when estimating the likelihood of uncertain events. The representativeness heuristic, availability heuristic, simulation heuristic, and the anchoring and adjustment heuristics are all described.

Learning Objectives

- Define and provide an example of the representativeness heuristic, the availability heuristic, the simulation heuristic, and the anchoring and adjustment heuristic.

Understanding Terminology

Match the terms on the right to the definitions/examples on the left.

______ 1. Making estimates by the ease in which you can picture it happening.	a. heuristics
______ 2. Quick estimates that save time and mental imagery.	b. representativeness heuristic
______ 3. Making estimates by ease in which cases come to mind.	c. availability heuristic
______ 4. Making estimates by using a starting point and then adjusting from that point.	d. simulation heuristic
______ 5. Making estimates based on how much it resembles the typical case.	e. anchoring and adjustment

Summary

Use the appropriate terms to complete each summary.

1. People use ___________________ to take shortcuts when making estimates. For example, if someone says they are afraid of flying because they believe flying is more dangerous than driving, they are probably making use of the ___________________ . Judging that someone is a librarian when all you know is that they like to read and wear glasses is using the ___________________ , as the person is statistically more likely to be a police officer than a librarian.

Section 4: Errors and Biases

Snapshot

Individuals have a number of errors and biases in their social thinking. For example, people tend to overestimate the number of people who share their beliefs and opinions but underestimate the number of people who have the same talents and abilities.

Learning Objectives

❖ Define and explain the following cognitive errors and biases: confirmation bias, conjunction fallacy, illusory correlation, base rate fallacy, gambler's fallacy, false consensus effect, false uniqueness effect, statistical regression, illusion of control, magical thinking, counterfactual thinking.

Understanding Terminology

Match the terms on the right to the definitions/examples on the left.

______ 1. E.g., believing the next coin flip will be heads, because the last three were tails.	a. conjunction fallacy
______ 2. Specificity leads to an expectation that it is more likely, when the opposite is true.	b. magical thinking
______ 3. The more common type of imagining alternative scenarios.	c. information overload
______ 4. Seeking information that will "prove" what you already believe to be true.	d. contamination
______ 5. Imagining other alternative scenarios.	e. false uniqueness effect
______ 6. After an extreme score, the subsequent score is usually closer to the mean.	f. false consensus effect
______ 7. Having too much information to possibly be able to integrate it all.	g. downward counterfactuals
______ 8. Imagining worse scenarios than what really happened.	h. illusion of control
______ 9. Everyone has the same attitudes as me.	i. confirmation bias
______ 10. Believing that wearing lucky socks will effect the outcome of the game.	j. upward counterfactuals
______ 11. Focusing on distinctive features and ignoring what is generally true.	k. gambler's fallacy
______ 12. Thinking that is illogical.	l. counterfactual thinking
______ 13. Causes disgust.	m. illusory correlation
______ 14. I am the only one who is this good at organic chemistry.	n. first instinct fallacy
______ 15. The belief that a first answer is better than changing to a new answer.	o. statistical regression
______ 16. Overestimating relationships between variables when little or none exists.	p. base rate fallacy

Summary

Use the appropriate terms to complete each summary.

1. ____________________ occurs when we seek information that confirms what we already believe and ignore information that disconfirms our existing beliefs. Other errors in thinking include the ____________________ which is when we fail to take into account or we underuse base rate information. Another error in thinking is that it is more likely that someone lives in a little house with cute flowerboxes out front than that someone lives in just a little house. This is called the ____________________.

2. People often overestimate how much other people share their beliefs or opinions and underestimate how many other people share their talents or successes. The former is called ____________________; the latter is called ____________________.

3. Believing that a coin flip will turn out heads because the last three coin flips landed tails is an example of ____________________ . Believing that blowing on the coin before it is flipped will help it land heads in an example of ____________________.

Section 5: Are People Really Idiots?

Snapshot

Although people do make many errors in thinking, many of these errors are self-correcting or not all that important. Some researchers have argued that for important decisions, people make fewer errors because they are more likely to use the conscious system. Further, cognitive errors can be reduced through effortful training.

Learning Objectives

- Explain how serious the errors heuristics and other decision making biases are for people.
- Describe some ways of reducing cognitive errors.

Summary

Use the appropriate terms to complete each summary.

1. People make fewer errors when they use ____________________ processing rather than ____________________ processing. This is called ____________________ .

Section 6: What Makes Us Human? Putting the Cultural Animal in Perspective

Snapshot

Complex thinking and the errors and biases in thinking are generally unique to animals.

Learning Objectives

- Explain how the complex thinking processes are unique to cultural animals.

Summary

Use the appropriate terms to complete each summary.

1. The capacity to use ___________________ allows humans to have complex patterns of thought. It also results in the use of ___________________ that leads to many errors and biases.

CHAPTER TEST

Multiple Choice Questions

1. What might a social psychologist call a person who doesn't like to think too hard or too long?
   a. cognitive miser
   b. lazy
   c. automatic thinker
   d. heuristic

2. John sees the word "red" in blue ink. When asked to state the color of the ink, he says "red." Why?
   a. He is a poor reader.
   b. His automatic thinking is difficult to override.
   c. The knowledge structure for red is well developed.
   d. Controlled thinking is too powerful.

3. You want to ride the elevator to the 7th floor. You walk up and push the up button. You then wait for the elevator to arrive and the doors to open. You walk in, turn around, and hit the button for floor 5. Thinking about scripts, what is the most likely explanation for this mistake?
   a. Your office is on the 5th floor, and that is where you usually take the elevator.
   b. You are not very elevator savvy.
   c. You are nervous because of other people in the elevator.
   d. The availability heuristic was applied.

4. In a study by Herman and Mack (1975), they randomly assigned participants to have one milkshake, two milkshakes, or no milkshakes. Then participates were asked to taste and then rate a number of different ice creams. Some participants were on diets and others were not. Which statement best summarizes the findings?
   a. Dieters, no matter the condition, ate the least ice cream.
   b. Non-dieters and dieters, no matter the condition, ate the same amount of ice cream.
   c. Nondieters ate the most ice cream if they didn't have any milkshakes, but otherwise dieters and non-dieters looked the same.
   d. Nondieters ate the most ice cream if they didn't have any milkshakes, but otherwise dieters ate more ice cream.

5. Hala has the ball with five seconds remaining in the basketball game. Her team is down by one point. She shoots the ball and after bouncing around the rim it falls in. Her team wins the game. After the game, she credits her success to how hard she worked all week in practice. However, last week when she missed a similar shot, she said she was unlucky. What does this scenario demonstrate?
a. fundamental attribution error
b. consistency
c. self-serving bias
d. actor/observer bias

6. Standing in line at the grocery store you are terribly annoyed and frustrated by the length of the line. You cannot believe how unlucky you were to get into the slow line. Just then, you notice the person in front of you acting very impatient and frustrated. You think to yourself, "what a grouch!" What does this scenario demonstrate?
a. fundamental attribution error
b. consistency
c. self-serving bias
d. actor/observer bias

7. Samir is wearing sunglasses on a rainy day. You wonder to yourself, why would he being wearing sunglasses? The sun isn't shining. You ask yourself, does he always where sunglasses on rainy days like this? According to Kelley's covariation principle, what type of information are you seeking?
a. consistency
b. consensus
c. distinctiveness
d. self-serving

8. Explaining poverty by saying that all poor people are lazy is an example of
a. the self-serving bias.
b. consensus.
c. the ultimate attribution error.
d. the actor/observer bias.

9. Which heuristic best explains why USC fans would be more upset after losing to UCLA by three points after a back and forth game than they would be after losing by 21 points?
a. availability
b. simulation
c. representativeness
d. anchoring and adjustment

10. Most people guess that Rebecca is a veterinarian because she lives on a farm, loves animals, and people call her “doctor.” However, she is a dentist. Which heuristic are people using when they assume she is a veterinarian?
a. availability
b. simulation
c. representativeness
d. anchoring and adjustment

11. Many Americans fear that they may die in a terrorist attack. However, statistically, people are much more likely to die in a car accident. Which heuristic explains this?
a. availability
b. simulation
c. representativeness
d. anchoring and adjustment

12. If you first ask participants whether the Nile is longer or shorter than 10,000 miles and then ask students to estimate the length of the Nile river, they will give estimates much higher than another group that was first asked whether the Nile is longer or shorter than 2,000 miles. Why?
a. availability
b. simulation
c. representativeness
d. anchoring and adjustment

13. Men report having many more sex partner than women. How can this be explained considering that men and women are having sex with one another?
a. Men are having sex with prostitutes and prostitutes are rarely surveyed.
b. Gay men are having more sex than lesbians and thus inflating the numbers for men more generally.
c. Answers may be distorted in opposite directions because men are motivated to appear virile and women are motivated to appear chaste.
d. All of the above may help explain the gender differences reported.

14. Have you ever gone to a restaurant and just loved the meal so much that you told all of your friends and couldn’t wait to return? Then, when you returned the next time, the food didn’t seem quite as wonderful. What might explain this experience?
a. magical thinking
b. false consensus effect
c. illusion of control
d. regression to the mean

15. At the end of the semester, you find out that you missed an A by just one point. What type of thinking are you likely to engage in?
a. regression to the mean
b. upward counterfactuals
c. downward counterfactuals
d. first instinct thinking

16. People often think that the phone always rings right when they are ready to walk out the door. What is this an example of?
a. illusory correlation
b. conjunction fallacy
c. illusion of control
d. bad luck

17. Which of the following is not a way to debias individuals?
a. Encourage people to use explicit decision rules.
b. Encourage people to consider multiple alternatives.
c. Encourage people to rely on their initial gut feeling.
d. Encourage people to use metacognition.

18. In what situation are people most likely to avoid the use of heuristics and use controlled processes?
a. when they are in a hurry
b. in matters of survival and reproduction
c. in matters of complex mathematical estimations
d. when it about an exam question

19. I am one of the only people who eats healthy, doesn't smoke, and goes to the gym. This is an example of what?
a. base rate fallacy
b. false consensus effect
c. false uniqueness effect
d. statistical regression

20. People spend a lot of time thinking. What topic do people spend the most time thinking about?
a. sex
b. work
c. people
d. what's for dinner

True or False Questions

T F 1. It is easy to suppress thoughts.

T F 2. People are likely to use conscious thinking when something violates their expectations.

T F 3. People do not make internal attributions for behavior that they know wasn't freely chosen.

T F 4. People generally make an external attribution when consensus, consistency, and distinctiveness are all high.

T F 5. Heuristics are mental shortcuts people use when making estimates.

T F 6. ESP can be explained with the anchor and adjustment heuristic.

T F 7. Confirmation bias means being skeptical of all information whether it supports your beliefs or not.

T F 8. If you are spending time thinking about "what might have been" you are engaging in counterfactual thinking.

T F 9. Information that is easier to understand results in improved decision making.

T F 10. Both humans and non-human animals appear to engage in counterfactual thinking.

Short Essay Questions

1. What are knowledge structures, schemas, and scripts?

2. Describe the fundamental attribution error.

3. What is the difference between the gambler's fallacy and the illusion of control?

Suggested Readings

Ayton, P., & Fischer, I. (2004). The hot hand fallacy and the gambler's fallacy: Two faces of subjective randomness? *Memory & Cognition*, *32*(8), 1369-1378.

El Leithy, S., Brown, G., & Robbins, I. (2006). Counterfactual thinking and posttraumatic stress reactions. *Journal of Abnormal Psychology*, *115*(3), 629-635.

O'Sullivan, M. (2003). The fundamental attribution error in detecting deception: The boy-who-cried-wolf effect. *Personality and Social Psychology Bulletin*, *29*(10), 1316-1327.

Schleicher, S., & Gilbert, L. (2005). Heterosexual dating discourses among college students: Is there still a double standard? *Journal of College Student Psychotherapy*, *19*(3), 7-23.

Tentori, K., Bonini, N., & Osherson, D. (2004). The conjunction fallacy: A misunderstanding about conjunction? *Cognitive Science*, *28*(3), 467-477.

Answer Key

Section 1

Understanding Terminology

1. e	6. g
2. j	7. d
3. a	8. b
4. f	9. c
5. h	10. i

Summary

1. social cognition, evolved
2. right answer, preferred conclusion, pretty good answer, automatic, conscious
3. knowledge structures, scripts, schema

Section 2

Understanding Terminology

1.	h	6.	d
2.	j	7.	e
3.	i	8.	c
4.	a	9.	g
5.	b	10.	f

Summary

1. self-serving bias, internal, situational or external, fundamental attribution error
2. covariation principle, consensus, consistency, distinctiveness

Section 3

Understanding Terminology

1. d
2. a
3. c
4. e
5. b

Summary

1. heuristics, availability heuristic, representativeness heuristic

Section 4

Understanding Terminology

1. k
2. a
3. j
4. i
5. l
6. o
7. c
8. g
9. f
10. h
11. p
12. b
13. d
14. e
15. n
16. m

Summary

1. confirmation bias, base rate fallacy, conjunction fallacy
2. false consensus effect, false uniqueness effect
3. gambler's fallacy, illusion of control

Section 5

Summary

1. controlled, automatic, debiasing

Section 6

Summary

1. language, heuristics

Chapter Test

Multiple Choice

1. a (p. 148)
2. b (p. 149)
3. a (p. 152)
4. d (p. 155)
5. c (p. 157)
6. d (p. 158)
7. a (p. 159)
8. c (p. 158)
9. b (p. 162)
10. c (p. 161)
11. a (p. 161)
12. d (p. 163)
13. d (p. 166)
14. d (p. 170)
15. b (p. 172)
16. a (p. 167)
17. c (p. 175)
18. b (p. 175)
19. c (p. 169)
20. c (p. 147)

True or False

1. F (p. 154)
2. T (p. 151)
3. F (p. 158)
4. T (p. 159)
5. T (p. 161)
6. F (p. 162)
7. F (p. 165)
8. T (p. 172)
9. T (p. 175)
10. F (p. 177)

Short Essay

1. What are knowledge structures, schemas, and scripts?

- Knowledge Structures: organized packets of information stored in our memory.
- Schemas: a type of knowledge structure that contains information about a particular concept, its attributes, and its connections to other concepts.
- Scripts: a type of knowledge structure about how people behave under certain conditions. Scripts define situations and guide behavior.

2. Describe the fundamental attribution error.
   - The fundamental attribution error is the tendency to over rely on internal attributions when explaining another person's behavior.

3. What is the difference between the gambler's fallacy and the illusion of control?
   - The gambler's fallacy is that we think a future random event will be determined by the outcome of past random events. In other words, surely this baby will be a boy, the last three were girls. In reality, the gender of previous births has no effect on subsequent births.
   - The illusion of control is the belief that we can control events that we have no control over. For example, a person may think that if they wear their hat backwards while watching the game, their favorite player will have a better game.

CHAPTER 6 – EMOTION AND AFFECT

CHAPTER REVIEW

Section 1: What Is Emotion?

Snapshot

Researchers have many different terms that refer to emotion. Sometimes they are used interchangeably, other times researchers distinguish between them. Most important is to distinguish between conscious emotion and automatic affect. Conscious emotion is the unified feeling of which we are keenly aware. Automatic affect is the quick responses of liking or disliking something. This can occur withou our conscious awareness.

Learning Objectives

- ❖ Define emotion, mood and affect.
- ❖ Describe the difference between conscious emotion and automatic affect.
- ❖ Explain what anthropolinguistics tells us about the names we have for emotions

Understanding Terminology

Match the terms on the right to the definitions/examples on the left.

______ 1. E.g., a strong feeling of joy or anger.	a. anthropolinguistics
______ 2. A feeling state that is not specifically linked to an event or cause.	b. emotion
______ 3. A quick feeling toward something, may not be a strong unified feeling.	c. automatic affect
______ 4. Your evaluative reaction to something.	d. mood
______ 5. Studying what matters in a culture by studying their language.	e. conscious emotion
______ 6. Tends to be categorized along a good-bad dimension.	f. affect

Summary

Use the appropriate terms to complete each summary.

1. ___________________ is a feeling state that is not linked to any particular event, while ___________________ is a feeling state that is conscious and an evaluative reaction to a particular event.

2. Examining a cultures' language to understand what they find important is called ___________________ .

Section 2: Emotional Arousal

Snapshot

Emotions reside not only in the brain, but also in physical ways. Several competing theories explain how the mental and physical aspects of emotion are linked. These include the James-Lange Theory of Emotion, Cannon-Bard Theory of Emotion, Schacter-Singer Theory of Emotion, and misattribution of arousal.

Learning Objectives

- ❖ Describe the differences between the James-Lange, Cannon-Bard, and Schacter-Singer theories of emotion.
- ❖ Define the facial feedback hypothesis and describe what it tells us about the James-Lange theory of emotion.
- ❖ Describe how excitation transfer can lead to a misattribution of arousal.
- ❖ Explain the ambiguities associated with sexual arousal.

Understanding Terminology

Match the terms on the right to the definitions/examples on the left.

______ 1. Arousal plus label.	a. facial feedback hypothesis
______ 2. First your body reacts and then the mind perceives the bodily reaction as emotion.	b. Canon-Bard theory of emotion
______ 3. Theory of emotion that involves the thalamus, cortex, and hypothalamus.	c. James-Lange theory of emotion
______ 4. Fast heartbeat, fast breathing, and sweaty palms.	d. Schacter-Singer theory of emotion
______ 5. I am aroused from caffeine, but attribute the arousal to my date.	e. arousal
______ 6. E.g., smile and you will feel happy.	f. excitation transfer

Summary

Use the appropriate terms to complete each summary.

1. The __________________ Theory of Emotion argued that __________________ processes came first and then __________________ rise from the perception of these processes.

2. The __________________ Theory of Emotion states that the __________________ is the relay station for nerve impulses and simultaneously sends a message to the cerebral cortex which produces the feeling of __________________ and to the hypothalamus which produces physiological __________________ .

3. The __________________ theory suggests that physiological arousal is similar in all emotions, but that the __________________ label differs.

Section 3: Some Important Emotions

Snapshot

In this section you will learn about several important emotions including happiness, anger, guilt, and shame. The roots of happiness are discussed as well at its relation to one's health and the phenomena of the hedonic treadmill. The causes and effects of anger are discussed as well as a rebuttal to catharsis theory. Finally, guilt and shame are discussed and distinguished from one another.

Learning Objectives

- Define happiness, affect balance, and life satisfaction.
- Explain the objective roots of happiness
- Define the hedonic treadmill.
- Explain the subjective roots of happiness.
- Describe how happiness can be increased and its relation to health.
- Define anger and its effect on individuals.
- Describe the causes of anger.
- Explain the effect of hiding versus showing anger, including whether catharsis theory is accurate.
- Describe the difference between guilt and shame.
- Explain the effect of guilt on people's behaviors and relationships.

Understanding Terminology

Match the terms on the right to the definitions/examples on the left.

______ 1. An unpleasant emotion that occurs after one has acted wrongly.	a. catharsis
______ 2. Positive emotions minus negative emotions.	b. life satisfaction
______ 3. An internal emotion that is a response to threat or provocation.	c. hedonic treadmill
______ 4. Uneasiness if you are the favored side of an unfair world.	d. shame
______ 5. My life in general compared to what I want is quite good.	e. survivor guilt
______ 6. I shouldn't have done that, I am a bad person.	f. affect balance
______ 7. The belief that venting anger is positive for the psyche.	g. guilt
______ 8. People tend to not move too far from their usual level of happiness.	h. anger

Summary

Use the appropriate terms to complete each summary.

1. Happiness is sometimes measured with __________________, which is positive emotions minus negative emotions. __________________ is a general evaluation of one's life, expectations, and comparison to standards.

2. Anger is an __________________ emotion that is high in __________________ . As a result, anger often provokes people to action.

3. Guilt is an emotion that occurs because of a particular __________________ , while __________________ tends to spread to the whole person. Sometimes, people feel __________________ if they perceive they benefited from an unfair world.

Section 4: Why Do We Have Emotions?

Snapshot

Although emotions have some drawbacks (feeling bad, doing foolish things), generally emotions are very adaptive because they promote belongingness, promot action (sometimes), guide thinking and learning, and help us make decisions and choices. The broaden-and-build theory argues that positive emotions encourage personal growth and development that may prepare the person for later hard times. Further, positive emotions are associated with flexibility, creativity, and better problem solving.

Learning Objectives

- Explain how emotions promote belongingness, cause behavior, guide thinking, learning, decisions, and choices.
- Define the affect-as-emotion hypothesis, affective forecasting, and risk-as-feelings hypothesis.
- Describe how we use food to moderate mood.
- Describe how positive emotions influence attention and mind-set (the broaden-and-build theory), flexibility, creativity and problem-solving.

Understanding Terminology

Match the terms on the right to the definitions/examples on the left.

______	1. This must be good, I feel happy about it.	a. affective forecasting
______	2. I'd feel terrible if the worst outcome occurred, I think I will avoid this risk.	b. broaden-and-build theory
______	3. Making predictions about future emotions.	c. affect-as-information hypothesis
______	4. I am more aware and focused when in a positive mood.	d. risk-as-feeling hypothesis

Summary

Use the appropriate terms to complete each summary.

1. Emotions serve many adaptive functions. For example, emotions promote ________________ by making us feel good when we make connections with others and making us feel awful when social connections are broken.

2. Emotions also guide our thinking. The ________________ hypothesis states that we understand our thinking about something by evaluating how we feel about it. Emotions also guide our decisions through ________________. We tend to be good at predicting what emotion we'll feel, but terrible at predicting the intensity or duration of the felt emotion. Emotions also steer our decisions as we imagine worst case scenarios as predicted by the ________________ hypothesis.

Section 5: Individual Differences in Emotion

Snapshot

People across many different cultures recognize six basic emotions: anger, surprise, disgust, happiness, fear, and sadness. However, there are cross cultural differences in the way people express these emotions. Although there is a strong stereotype that women are more emotional than men, typically studies do not find gender differences in the experience of emotions.

Learning Objectives

- ❖ Explain how emotions are similar and different across cultures.
- ❖ Describe the differences (or lack thereof) between men and women in emotions.

Summary

Use the appropriate terms to complete each summary.

1. Paul Eckman argues that individuals across different cultures are able to ________________ six different emotions from facial expressions. However, James Russell argues that only in ________________ photos can people recognize these emotions, that people across cultures cannot recognize the emotions in spontaneous expressions.

2. Despite the ________________, men and women are remarkably alike when it comes to experiencing emotions.

Section 6: Arousal, Attention, and Performance

Snapshot

Too little and too much arousal can be harmful for performance. There appears to be an optimal amount of arousal that is beneficial for tasks and this varies dependi on the complexity of the task.

Learning Objectives

❖ Explain the effect of arousal on attention and performance.

Summary

Use the appropriate terms to complete each summary.

1. The ____________________ Law has found that the association between arousal and performance is in the shape of an inverted U. Arousal, in the right amount, may b beneficial because it ____________________ and ____________________ attention.

Section 7: Emotional Intelligence

Snapshot

Emotional intelligence (EQ) is the ability to perceive, access and generate, understand, and reflectively regulate emotions. Some evidence suggests that EQ associated with workplace and school success.

Learning Objectives

❖ Define emotional intelligence.

Summary

Use the appropriate terms to complete each summary.

1. ____________________ is distinct from IQ as it is about how able people are to perceive, generate, understand and regulate emotions.

Section 8: Affect Regulation

Snapshot

People regulate their affect through a number of different strategies. We assume people mostly want to eliminate negative emotions and generate or maintain positive emotions, but this is not the case. For example, people may desire a neutral mood when meeting new people which may require eliminating a good mood. There appears to be several consistent differences in the way men and women generally regulate moods; women are more likely to ruminate while men are more likely to look for a distraction.

Learning Objectives

- ❖ Describe the various affect regulation strategies.
- ❖ Describe the goals of affect regulation and why one might want to increase or decrease positive and negative affect.
- ❖ Explain the difference in emotion control strategies between men and women.

Summary

Use the appropriate terms to complete each summary.

1. Although ___________________ initially increases arousal, it eventually decreases arousal once tired and is considered a very good way to regulate affect. Another good way cheer oneself up is to spend time with ___________________.

2. Women are more likely to ___________________ when feeling depressed while men are more likely to try to ___________________ themselves. Further, women are more likely to ___________________ and men are more likely to ___________________ to regulate mood.

Section 9: What Makes Us Human? Putting the Cultural Animal in Perspective

Snapshot

In humans, emotions are particularly important because they are tied to ideas, meanings, and cognitions.

Learning Objectives

- ❖ Describe how emotion and emotion regulation is uniquely human.

Summary

Use the appropriate terms to complete each summary.

1. Humans may be the only animal to have developed __________________ which includes the power to regulate emotions.

CHAPTER TEST

Multiple Choice Questions

1. In a study of the most common emotion words recalled by participants, 11 of 12 countries had ___
   a. more positive words than negative.
   b. more negative words than positive.
   c. an equal number of both positive and negative words.
   d. too many emotion words to analyze.

2. Joan just found out that she has been given a pay raise and a promotion. She is experiencing a lot of joy as a result of the news. What term, according to the text, is the best label for her experience?
   a. mood
   b. affect
   c. emotion
   d. automatic affect

3. Which theory of emotion predicts that you are more likely to feel happy if you put a smile on your face?
   a. Universal Theory of Emotion
   b. Schachter-Singer Theory of Emotion
   c. Cannon-Bard Theory of Emotion
   d. James-Lange Theory of Emotion

4. After seeing a scary movie, I find myself feeling more "in love" with my date. What can best explain this experience?
   a. passion
   b. excitation transfer
   c. the work of the thalamus
   d. facial feedback

5. Which of the following is not an objective predictor of happiness?
   a. having children
   b. money
   c. a happy marriage
   d. a good job

6. Research has shown that people can increase their general level of happiness in a variety of ways. Which of the following increases happiness?
   a. being optimistic
   b. forgiving others
   c. being grateful for good things
   d. all of the above can increase happiness

7. Emotions can be grouped by two important dimensions. What are these important dimensions?
   a. arousal and pleasantness
   b. arousal and intensity
   c. duration and pleasantness
   d. duration and intensity

8. Jenny is trying to decide if she wants to go to Spain for the summer. She thinks, "I'm sure this will make me very happy" and decides to go. What concept does this exemplify?
   a. build-and-broaden theory
   b. affect-as-information hypothesis
   c. risk-as-feeling hypothesis
   d. smile-be-happy hypothesis

9. Javier is considering changing his major to art. However, he envisions a future in which he cannot find a job and is unable to support himself. He then decides to keep his finance major. What concept does this illustrate?
   a. build-and-broaden theory
   b. affect-as-information hypothesis
   c. risk-as-feeling hypothesis
   d. smile-be-happy hypothesis

10. Which of the following is associated with good moods?
   a. creativity
   b. persistence
   c. problem-solving ability
   d. all of the above

11. What is a Duchenne smile?
    a. a fake smile that is generally seen in posed photographs
    b. a smile that is seen when people are trying to hide anger or guilt
    c. a smile seen most often on people from collectivistic cultures
    d. a genuine smile that involves facial muscles and muscles around the eyes

12. If a student is under high stress while taking a test, which answer are they most likely to choose?
    a. A
    b. B
    c. C
    d. D

13. In which of the following scenarios, would high levels of arousal be most beneficial?
    a. trying a new gymnastics routine for the very first time
    b. doing a flip that you have completed thousands of time
    c. doing a complicated double reverse twist-around dismount
    d. all of the above would benefit from high levels of arousal

14. The four branches of emotional intelligence are believed to be ordered from the more basic process to higher-order processes. Which of the following answer choices is ordered from the most basic to the most higher-order process?
    a. understand, perceive, generate, regulate
    b. perceive, understand, generate, regulate
    c. perceive, generate, understand, regulate
    d. generate, perceive, understand, regulate

15. Having high emotional intelligence has been linked with ___
    a. greater merit increases at work.
    b. problems forming close relationships.
    c. book smarts.
    d. having only positive emotions.

16. A.J. is depressed and finds that she can't stop thinking about the problem. What is this called?
    a. consummation
    b. effective regulation
    c. rumination
    d. affective fostering

17. James just found out he got an A in his social psychology class. He is in an excellent mood. He is now heading out to meet his new roommate. What is he likely to do before meeting his new roommate?
a. to maintain is good mood by calling his sister to tell her
b. to shift his mood to neutral through thinking about something sad
c. to ruminate about his success
d. to go get a drink

18. Although people find different strategies of mood regulation effective, in general, research finds that ___ is most effective.
a. sleep
b. reframing
c. distraction
d. exercise

19. Emotions play a particularly large role in human life because they are uniquely linked to all of the following in humans except ___
a. ideas.
b. meanings.
c. cognitions.
d. hunger.

20. In an important study by Schacter and Singer, participants were either given a shot of adrenaline or a saline solution before being exposed to a confederate who was acting either very happy or angry. Half of the participants who were given adrenaline were told that they were given adrenaline and that it would make their heart beat faster among other "side affects." What did this study find?
a. Only participants who were given adrenaline shots joined in the emotional experience of the confederate.
b. Only participants who were given saline shots joined in the emotional experience of the confederate.
c. Only participants who were given adrenaline but not told of the "side effects" joined in the emotional experience of the confederate.
d. Receiving adrenaline or saline had no effect of the participants emotional experience.

True or False Questions

T F 1. People can experience automatic affect for things they have never even encountered before.

T F 2. According to the Cannon-Bard Theory of Emotion, the hypothalamus is the relay center that is important to physiology and emotion.

T F 3. Research has found that men who say they are opposed to gay sex were the most aroused by gay sex, even though they said they were not.

T F 4. People are generally much happier a year after winning the lottery than right before winning.

T F 5. It is generally unhealthy to conceal anger for the long-term

T F 6. Researchers believe that guilt may be an important functional emotion.

T F 7. Research has found that bad mood may be a better predictor of how much a person eats than hunger.

T F 8. Women, as expected, tend to be much more emotional than men.

T F 9. According to the Yerkes-Dodson Law, a basketball player would benefit from more arousal when shooting a lay-up as opposed to a three-pointer.

T F 10. Seeking out friends to eliminate negative emotion usually fails because you just infect your friends with your bad mood.

Short Essay Questions

1. Define emotion and explain three different views on how emotion and arousal are linked.

2. Describe how guilt and shame are different emotions.

3. How does the risk-as-feeling hypothesis impact our decision making?

Suggested Readings

Brackett, M., Rivers, S., Shiffman, S., Lerner, N., & Salovey, P. (2006). Relating emotional abilities to social functioning: A comparison of self-report and performance measures of emotional intelligence. *Journal of Personality and Social Psychology*, *91*(4), 780-795.

Conway, A. (2005). Girls, aggression, and emotion regulation. *American Journal of Orthopsychiatry*, *75*(2), 334-339.

Dickerson, S., Kemeny, M., Aziz, N., Kim, K., & Fahey, J. (2004). Immunological effects of induced shame and guilt. *Psychosomatic Medicine*, *66*(1), 124-131.

Matsumoto, D. (2006). Are cultural differences in emotion regulation mediated by personality traits? *Journal of Cross-Cultural Psychology*, *37*(4), 421-437.

Sim, L., & Zeman, J. (2006). The contribution of emotion regulation to body dissatisfaction and disordered eating in early adolescent girls. *Journal of Youth and Adolescence*, *35*(2), 219-228.

Answer Key

Section 1

Understanding Terminology

1. e
2. d
3. c
4. b
5. a
6. f

Summary

1. mood, emotion
2. anthropolinguistic

Section 2

Understanding Terminology

1. d
2. c
3. b
4. e
5. f
6. a

Summary

1. James-Lange, bodily, emotions
2. Cannon-Bard, thalamus, emotion, arousal
3. Schachter-Singer, cognitive

Section 3

Understanding Terminology

1. g
2. f
3. h
4. e
5. b
6. d
7. a
8. c

Summary

1. affect balance, life satisfaction
2. unpleasant, arousal
3. action, shame, survivor guilt

Section 4

Understanding Terminology

1. c
2. d
3. a
4. b

Summary

1. belongingness
2. affect-as-information, affective forecasting, risk-as-feeling

Section 5

Summary

1. recognize, posed
2. stereotype

Section 6

Summary

1. Yerkes-Dodson, narrows, focuses

Section 7

Summary

1. emotional intelligence

Section 8

Summary

1. exercise, friends
2. ruminate, distract, eat, drink

Section 9

Summary

1. emotional intelligence

Chapter Test

Multiple Choice

1. b (p. 184)
2. c (p. 183)
3. d (p. 185)
4. b (p. 187)
5. a (p. 191)
6. d (p. 193)
7. a (p. 194)
8. b (p. 203)
9. c (p. 205)
10. d (p. 206)
11. d (p. 207)
12. a (p. 212)
13. b (p. 211)
14. c (p. 213)
15. a (p. 213)
16. c (p. 216)
17. b (p. 215)
18. d (p. 215)
19. d (p. 218)
20. c (p. 187)

True or False

1. T (p. 183)
2. F (p. 186)
3. T (p. 188)
4. F (p. 192)
5. T (p. 196)
6. T (p. 198)
7. T (p. 202)
8. F (p. 209)
9. T (p. 211)
10. F (p. 214)

Short Essay

1. Define emotion and explain three different views on how emotion and arousal are linked.
   - Emotion is a conscious evaluative reaction to something. Examples include anger, happiness, guilt, sadness.
     - James-Lange Theory
     - Cannon-Bard Theory
     - Schacter-Singer Theory

2. Describe how guilt and shame are different emotions.
   - Guilt refers to a negative emotion experienced if you perceive you have acted badly or wrongly.
   - Shame, like guilt, is a negative emotion, but it spreads to the whole person.

3. How does the risk-as-feeling hypothesis impact our decision making?
   - Our decision making is impacted when we allow our emotional responses to a worst case scenario bias our judgments and decision making.

CHAPTER 7 – ATTITUDES, BELIEFS, AND CONSISTENCY

CHAPTER REVIEW

Section 1: What are attitudes and why do people have them?

Snapshot

Attitudes are our evaluative reactions toward things, ideas, and people. Attitudes exist both on the implicit and explicit level. Implicit attitudes are unconscious and uncontrollable evaluations. Explicit attitudes are conscious and controllable. Attitudes help make sense of a complex social world and often direct our choices and behavior.

Learning Objectives

- ❖ Differentiate attitude and belief.
- ❖ Describe dual attitudes.
- ❖ Define stigma.
- ❖ Explain what attitudes do for people.
- ❖ Explain the effect of optimism and pessimism on people's lives.

Understanding Terminology

Match the terms on the right to the definitions/examples on the left.

______ 1. Holding two attitudes that may not be consistent.	a. attitudes
______ 2. Bits of information, opinions, or facts.	b. explicit attitudes
______ 3. Uncontrollable and unconscious attitudes.	c. stigma
______ 4. Controllable and conscious attitudes.	d. beliefs
______ 5. Favorable or unfavorable evaluations of an object or issues.	e. implicit attitudes
______ 6. An attribute about a social group that generally invokes a negative attitude.	f. dual attitudes

Summary

Use the appropriate terms to complete each summary.

1. ____________________ help us explain the world, while ____________________ help us make choices. Sometimes we may have different or contrasting attitudes toward the same thing which is called ____________________. This may be because of our ____________________ mind in which we have unconscious attitudes that are called ____________________ and more controlled conscious attitudes that are called ____________________ .

Section 2: How Attitudes are Formed

Snapshot

Attitudes are formed in a number of ways including mere exposure, classical conditioning, operant conditioning, and social learning. Additionally, existing attitudes may become more polarized after thinking about them.

Learning Objectives

- Describe the effect of repeated exposure on liking, as well as define the mere exposure effect.
- Explain how classical conditioning works.
- Define operant conditioning and social learning.
- Describe the effect of polarization on attitudes.

Understanding Terminology

Match the terms on the right to the definitions/examples on the left.

______ 1. The way a neutral stimulus comes to be liked or disliked.	a. unconditioned response
______ 2. The response that has been learned through repeated pairings.	b. conditioned stimulus
______ 3. A response that needed no learning.	c. mere exposure effect
______ 4. Reward = more likely; punishment = less likely.	d. social learning
______ 5. A stimulus that through repeated pairings now elicits a particular response.	e. neutral stimulus
______ 6. After seeing the picture every day, I like it.	f. operant conditioning
______ 7. A stimulus that initially evokes no response.	g. classical conditioning
______ 8. Learning through watching others receive reward or punishment.	h. conditioned response
______ 9. Something that evokes a response without any learning.	i. attitude polarization
______ 10. Movement toward more extreme attitudes after reflecting on them.	j. unconditioned stimulus

Summary

Use the appropriate terms to complete each summary.

1. __________________ can be formed in many different ways. Some attitudes are formed through __________________ (seeing something over and over). Other times, attitudes may arise after a neutral stimulus is paired with something that you already like or dislike. This is called __________________. Further, operant conditioning may help us form attitudes as we are likely to form positive attitudes about things that are associated with __________________ and negative attitudes about things that are associated with __________________. Finally, some attitudes may be formed through observing others. This is called __________________.

2. Attitudes often tend to __________________ upon reflection, possibly because we consider new information and apply biases.

Section 3: Consistency

Snapshot

People generally prefer consistency in their attitudes and behaviors. Heider's balance theory argues that we prefer balance among our unit and sentiment relationships. Cognitive dissonance theory argues that inconsistency between our attitudes and behaviors produces psychological discomfort and that we will either justify our behavior or change our attitude to reduce dissonance.

Learning Objectives

- ❖ Explain balanced and unbalanced states in Heider's P-O-X theory.
- ❖ Explain the effect of cognitive dissonance on attitude change.
- ❖ Describe how effort justification relates to cognitive dissonance and affects attitudes.
- ❖ Describe how experimenters could induce individuals to choose to do something they have a negative attitude toward.
- ❖ Explain the important factors in creating change within cognitive dissonance.

Understanding Terminology

Match the terms on the right to the definitions/examples on the left.

_____ 1. E.g., I like sweaters.	a. balance theory
_____ 2. P-O-X theory.	b. cognitive dissonance
_____ 3. This inconsistency is bothersome, I'll change my attitude.	c. unit relationships
_____ 4. I must like calculus, I worked so hard in the class.	d. sentiment relationships
_____ 5. E.g., Charlie owns a Toyota.	e. effort justification

Summary

Use the appropriate terms to complete each summary.

1. I like Suzie; Suzie likes Chinese food; I dislike Chinese food. According to __________________ theory, this set of relationships is __________________.

2. If I believe that smoking is harmful, but still smoke a pack a day, I should feel psychological __________________ according to __________________ theory. Further, I should either change my __________________ or justify my __________________ to eliminate the inconsistency.

Section 4: Do Attitudes Predict Behavior

Snapshot

Attitudes predict behavior, but only under certain conditions. Specific attitudes predict behavior; attitudes predict aggregated behavior; general attitudes that are put into context predict behavior; and accessible attitudes predict behavior.

Learning Objectives

- ❖ Describe the debate about whether attitudes predict behaviors, including the defense offered by those who believe there is a connection.
- ❖ Describe how the A-B problem is related to sex.

Summary

Use the appropriate terms to complete each summary.

1. Although often there is no link between attitudes and behaviors (called the ___________________), attitudes have been found to predict behavior when the attitude measured is ___________________. Further, our attitudes may not predict a specific behavior at a specific time, but may predict ___________________ behavior.

2. Attitudes are also more predictive of behavior if you help a person understand the connection between an attitude and a behavior. This is putting an attitude in ___________________. Finally, attitudes that easily come to mind or are ___________________ are more likely to predict behavior.

Section 5: Beliefs and Believing

Snapshot

Research has found that we believe everything we understand, at least until we can consciously reject the idea. Thus, when people are busy or tired, they are more likely to believe things. Further, once beliefs have formed, they are quite resistant to change. Our beliefs about the world may play an important part in how we cope with trauma.

Learning Objectives

- Explain the connection between understanding and believing.
- Describe how belief perseverance works.
- Explain how assumptive worlds are affected by traumatic events and the implications of that for coping with such events.
- Describe why people have religious beliefs and irrational beliefs.

Understanding Terminology

Match the terms on the right to the definitions/examples on the left.

_____ 1. Our world is what we believe it to be.	a. assumptive worlds
_____ 2. Sticking with a held belief, even if it no longer has factual support.	b. coping
_____ 3. What we believe is very important in how we handle stress and trauma.	c. downward comparison
_____ 4. If I compare myself to you, I will feel better because you are worse off than me.	d. belief perseverance
_____ 5. The way we manage stress to return to normal functioning.	e. cognitive coping

Summary

Use the appropriate terms to complete each summary.

1. Research has found that beliefs ___________________ even when the information on which they have been formed is discredited.

2. We hold beliefs about the world, which Janoff-Bulman referred to as ___________________. These beliefs must be restored before people can effectively ___________________ with trauma. This restoration of beliefs is called ___________________ by Shelley Taylor. One way we do this is by thinking "it could have been worse" which is called ___________________.

CHAPTER TEST

Multiple Choice Questions

1. Winston thinks that most milking cows are black and white. This is Winston's ___
   a. attitude.
   b. belief.
   c. implicit attitude.
   d. explicit attitude.

2. Maria prefers bowling over putt-putt golf. This reflects Maria's ___
   a. stigma.
   b. dual attitude.
   c. belief.
   d. attitude.

3. When comparing the IAT to more traditional survey measures of attitudes toward stigmatized groups, it is typically found that ___ attitudes are more negative than ___ attitudes.
   a. dual; explicit
   b. explicit; implicit
   c. implicit; explicit
   d. implicit; dual

4. Which of the following individuals would you predict to live a long and healthy life?
   a. John who is not a pessimist.
   b. Juan who is an optimist.
   c. Jean who both a pessimist and an optimist.
   d. No prediction, all would have the same likelihood of living a long and healthy life.

5. Mitsue's mother serves the same meal every Friday evening. Mitsue originally did not care one way or the other about the meal, but now finds that she really enjoys it. This is an example of ___
   a. social learning.
   b. operant conditioning.
   c. classical conditioning.
   d. the mere exposure effect.

6. Samir's father serves lamb chops with couscous, which Samir does not care for very much. If Samir eats his meal, he is rewarded with TV time. Over time, Samir finds that he does in fact like lamb chops and couscous. This is an example of ___
a. social learning.
b. operant conditioning.
c. classical conditioning.
d. the mere exposure effect.

7. Jimmy notices how his big sister loves doing her homework and is praised by their parents. Jimmy also begins to love doing his homework. This is an example of ___
a. social learning.
b. operant conditioning.
c. classical conditioning.
d. the mere exposure effect.

8. Sarah has always thought that women should have equal opportunities to men. Once arriving at college, Sarah enrolled in a sociology class that made her think about her beliefs about gender. Which of the following was a likely consequence of her thinking?
a. Sarah became more extreme in her feminist ideas.
b. Sarah became less extreme in her feminist ideas.
c. Sarah's attitude toward equality did not change.
d. Sarah changed her mind completely.

9. If I endure a difficult initiation to become a member of a fraternity, I will likely have a very ___ attitude toward the group.
a. negative
b. positive
c. neutral
d. split

10. In Festinger's classic study of cognitive dissonance, which group of participants showed the most attitude change?
a. Those that did not tell the lie.
b. Those that had been paid $20 to lie about how enjoyable the experiment was.
c. Those that had only been paid $1 to lie about how enjoyable the experiment was.
d. Those that thought the activity was fun from the beginning.

11. Which of the following is balanced according to P-O-X theory?
    a. I like Sue; I like Laura; Laura does not like Sue.
    b. I am dating Huy; Huy likes roller coasters; I do not like roller coasters.
    c. I hate jelly; I hate Samantha; Samantha likes jelly.
    d. I dislike Sharon; Sharon dislikes Matt; I dislike Matt.

12. In the study by Comer and Laird in which they asked some students to eat worms, what did they find?
    a. Fewer than 20% of students had favorable attitudes toward worm eating.
    b. Some students who were given a chance to switch to worm eating, did so.
    c. Worm eating was so disgusting to most students, there was little change in attitudes.
    d. If students expected having to eat a worm, many changed their attitudes toward the task. Then when given an escape, 80% still ate the worm.

13. Natasha thinks that democracy is important in the general sense, but didn't vote in the last election. Why might there be this inconsistency?
    a. Liking democracy is a general attitude and may not predict specific voting behavior.
    b. She may have voted in other elections, but have been out of town on the last election.
    c. She may rarely think about her pro-democracy attitudes.
    d. All of the above can explain the attitude-behavior inconsistency.

14. What is the inconsistency between attitudes and behaviors called?
    a. the A-B problem
    b. dissonance problem
    c. P-O-X problem
    d. existential problem

15. LaPiere found that most business owners in 1934 reported that they would not serve Chinese people. When LaPiere and a Chinese couple went to these actual establishments, what happened?
    a. Most refused service to the Chinese couple.
    b. Fifty percent of the business owners actually provided service to Chinese couple.
    c. All but one of the business owners provided service to the Chinese couple.
    d. All refused service to the Chinese couple.

16. Who stated that attitudes are the most important concept in Social Psychology?
a. Leon Festinger
b. Gordon Allport
c. Roy Baumeister
d. Alan Wicker

17. In a classic study, it was found that people who read that risk-taking people make better firefighters than cautious people believed this even after being told that the information was bogus. How can this belief perseverance be eliminated?
a. Remind participants that the information was bogus again and again.
b. Tell the participants that the researchers do not know anything about firefighters.
c. Ask participants to think of reasons why cautious people might make better firefighters.
d. None of the above would counteract belief perseverance.

18. Which of the following is not one of the three main beliefs called assumptive worlds?
a. God exists.
b. I am a good person.
c. The world is benevolent.
d. The world is fair and just.

19. The phrase "it could have been a lot worse" is indicative of ___
a. upward comparison.
b. downward comparison.
c. the lucky me belief.
d. irrational beliefs.

20. Which is an automatic process?
a. believing
b. disbelieving
c. coping
d. downward comparisons

True or False Questions

T F 1. According to the text, people only have attitudes about very important things.

T F 2. Attitudes help us seek reward and avoid punishment.

T F 3. In classical conditioning, punishment and reward is very important.

T F 4. Most people prefer their own mirror image, but the true image of friends.

T F 5. You are much more likely to feel dissonance if your inconsistent behavior is public than if it is private.

T F 6. Women who experienced an unpleasant initiation into a group, rated the (very boring) group more interesting than women who had a pleasant initiation.

T F 7. Men have a stronger correlation between sexual attitudes and sexual behavior than women.

T F 8. Specific attitudes are better at predicting behavior than general attitudes.

T F 9. People who hold irrational beliefs are more likely to become depressed and have lower levels of self-esteem.

T F 10. People recover more slowly from sexual assault if they use religion to cope.

Short Essay Questions

1. When is there a link between attitudes and behavior?

2. Describe cognitive dissonance theory.

3. Can blaming oneself ever be a good way to cope with trauma?

Suggested Readings

Baumeister, R. (2004). Gender and erotic plasticity: Sociocultural influences on the sex drive. *Sexual and Relationship Therapy*, *19*(2), 133-139.

Gosling, P., Denizeau, M., & Oberlé, D. (2006). Denial of responsibility: A new mode of dissonance reduction. *Journal of Personality and Social Psychology*, *90*(5), 722-733.

Parsons, S., Cruise, P., Davenport, W., & Jones, W. (2006). Religious beliefs, practices and treatment adherence among individuals with HIV in the southern United States. *AIDS Patient Care and STDs*, *20*(2), 97-111.

Sinclair, S., Lowery, B., Hardin, C., & Colangelo, A. (2005). Social tuning of automatic racial attitudes: The role of affiliative motivation. *Journal of Personality and Social Psychology*, *89*(4), 583-592.

Stone, J., Aronson, E., Crain, A., & Winslow, M. (1994). Inducing hypocrisy as a means of encouraging young adults to use condoms. *Personality and Social Psychology Bulletin*, *20*(1), 116-128.

Answer Key

Section 1

Understanding Terminology

1. f
2. d
3. e
4. b
5. a
6. c

Summary

1. Beliefs, attitudes, dual attitudes, duplex, implicit attitudes, explicit attitudes

Section 2

Understanding Terminology

1.	g	6.	c
2.	h	7.	e
3.	a	8.	d
4.	f	9.	j
5.	b	10.	i

Summary

1. Attitudes, mere exposure, classical conditioning, reward, punishment, social learning
2. polarize

Section 3

Understanding Terminology

1. d
2. a
3. b
4. e
5. c

Summary

1. balance, unbalanced
2. discomfort, cognitive dissonance, attitudes, behavior

Section 4

Summary

1. A-B problem, specific, aggregated
2. context, accessible

Section 5

Understanding Terminology

1. a
2. d
3. e
4. c
5. b

Summary

1. persevere
2. assumptive worlds, cope, cognitive coping, downward comparison

Chapter Test

Multiple Choice

1.	b	(p. 226)	11.	c	(p.232)
2.	d	(p. 226)	12.	d	(p. 236)
3.	c	(p. 226)	13.	d	(p. 239)
4.	a	(p. 228)	14.	a	(p. 240)
5.	d	(p. 229)	15.	c	(p. 238)
6.	b	(p. 230)	16.	b	(p. 238)
7.	a	(p. 230)	17.	c	(p. 242)
8.	a	(p. 231)	18.	a	(p. 243)
9.	b	(p. 234)	19.	b	(p. 244)
10.	c	(p. 234)	20.	a	(p. 241)

True or False

1. F (p. 228)
2. T (p. 227)
3. F (p. 229)
4. T (p. 229)
5. T (p. 237)
6. T (p. 235)
7. F (p. 240)
8. T (p. 239)
9. T (p. 245)
10. F (p. 245)

Short Essay

1. When is there a link between attitudes and behavior?

    - Specific attitudes are measured.
    - Behavior is aggregated.
    - Behavior is put in context of attitude.
    - Attitude is accessible.

2. Describe cognitive dissonance theory.

    - There is an inconsistency between a person's held attitude and behavior. This causes psychological discomfort that the person is motivated to reduce. In order to reduce discomfort and restore consistency the person can either change their attitude or justify their behavior.

3. Can blaming oneself ever be a good way to cope with trauma?

    - Yes, if blaming oneself allows one to restore consistency between what happened and assumptive world beliefs, self-blame can be an effective coping strategy.

CHAPTER 8 – PROSOCIAL BEHAVIOR: DOING WHAT'S BEST FOR OTHERS

CHAPTER REVIEW

Section 1: What Is Prosocial Behavior?

Snapshot

Prosocial behavior includes a wide variety of behaviors including helping, conforming, obeying, and cooperating. Most prosocial behavior is in the service of building or maintaining personal relationships. Reciprocity and fairness norms dictate much prosocial behavior.

Learning Objectives

- Define prosocial behavior, what it involves, and its consequence for humans and society.
- Describe the human capacities for reciprocity and fairness.

Understanding Terminology

Match the terms on the right to the definitions/examples on the left.

_____ 1. You help me; I'll help you.	a. prosocial behavior
_____ 2. Everyone gets the same benefits no matter their contributions.	b. survivor guilt
_____ 3. A prescription for expected behavior.	c. rule of law
_____ 4. Worrying about one's relationships when outperforming others.	d. reciprocity
_____ 5. Guilty feelings for surviving when others didn't.	e. overbenefited
_____ 6. Doing things that help others or society at large.	f. norms
_____ 7. Receiving more benefits than one deserves according to contributions.	g. sensitivity about being a target of threatening upward comparison
_____ 8. Benefits are proportional to contributions.	h. equity
_____ 9. Receiving fewer benefits than one deserves according to contributions.	i. underbenefited
_____ 10. Describes a society in which the laws are followed.	j. equality

Summary

Use the appropriate terms to complete each summary.

1. ________________________ behavior is any behavior that is beneficial to others or society in general. Society's that have a strong ________________________ have more prosocial behavior.

2. If I do something for you, you are likely to return the favor because of the obligation of ________________________. People are also motivated by ________________________ that represent the standards established by a society to act in a certain way. Two norms are ________________________ and ________________________. A situation can be unfair because you received more than you deserved (________________________) or because you received less than you deserved (________________________).

Section 2: Your Fair Share

Snapshot

Research has shown that people will often take more than their fair share, even if it means an eventual elimination of the resource. This is referred to as the tragedy of the commons. Many variables appear to be associated with people selfishly hoarding resources or taking their fair share.

Learning Objectives

- ❖ Describe why the tragedy of the commons and hoarding occur and how to lesse them.

Summary

Use the appropriate terms to complete each summary.

1. Often, fish and other resources become depleted because people take more thar their fair share. This is called the ________________________. People are less likely to hoard if they communicate with each other, ________________________ one another, and share a ________________________ identity.

Section 3: Cooperation, Forgiveness, Obedience, and Conformity

Snapshot

This section reviews research on cooperation, forgiveness, obedience, and conformity. All of these concepts promote prosocial behavior and assist us in our quest to be accepted by others.

Learning Objectives

- Explain cooperation and the prisoner's dilemma.
- Differentiate a non-zero-sum game from a zero-sum game.
- Describe the effect of forgiveness on the forgiver and the forgiven.
- Explain the effect of positive and negative information on reputations or impressions.
- Explain Milgram's obedience experiment and what it teaches us about obedience.
- Describe conformity and how it is affected by normative and informational social influence.
- Compare public conformity and private attitude change.
- Describe conformity in the restaurant setting.

Understanding Terminology

Match the terms on the right to the definitions/examples on the left.

_____ 1. Doing what others are doing.	a. cooperation
_____ 2. A game that requires players to choose between being competitive or cooperative.	b. prisoner's dilemma
_____ 3. Letting go of anger or attempts to get even.	c. non-zero sum game
_____ 4. A game in which what I win you must lose and vice versa.	d. zero-sum game
_____ 5. Laughing at a joke, but thinking it is not funny.	e. private attitude change
_____ 6. Working together to accomplish a common goal.	f. public conformity
_____ 7. Coming to believe something different.	g. informational social influence
_____ 8. Doing what an authority figure tells you to do.	h. normative social influence
_____ 9. A game that everyone can win (or lose).	i. conformity
_____ 10. Going along because you think others have information that you can use.	j. obedience
_____ 11. Going along to get along.	k. forgiveness

Summary

Use the appropriate terms to complete each summary.

1. The ________________________ game allows players to choose between ________________________ and ________________________. It is a ________________________ game because both participants can win (or lose).

2. If you hurt me, but I choose to let go of my anger against you, I have ________________________ you. This is extremely important to romantic relationship success.

3. In a famous study by ________________________, an authority figure told participants to shock a "learner." This study illustrated ________________________.

4. In a famous study by ________________________, participants were instructed to select the longest line. However, the confederates all gave the wrong answer. It was found that many participants ________________________ by also giving the wrong answer.

Section 4: Why Do People Help Others?

Snapshot

People help others for several reasons. From an evolutionary perspective, we help our relatives because they share some of our genes. We also help others if we feel empathy for them because we want to reduce their distress. Finally, we may help others for egoistical reasons such as personal gain or reward.

Learning Objectives

- Explain the evolutionary benefits of helping.
- Contrast egoistic helping and altruistic helping.
- Explain the connection between altruistic helping and empathy.

Understanding Terminology

Match the terms on the right to the definitions/examples on the left.

_____ 1. Helping others because there is a benefit for ourselves.	a. empathy-altruism hypothesis
_____ 2. E.g., if you are sad, I am sad.	b. kin selection
_____ 3. Altruistic helping increases when a person feels empathy.	c. negative state relief theory
_____ 4. Helping another with no expectation of reward or benefit.	d. empathy
_____ 5. The explanation for why we are more likely to help a brother than a cousin.	e. egoistic helping
_____ 6. Helping others to relieve our own distress.	f. altruistic helping

Summary

Use the appropriate terms to complete each summary.

1. Helping another person for personal gain is called ________________________ . Helping another person with no expectation of a reward or benefit is called ________________________. The ________________________ hypothesis has garnered more support than the competing ________________________ theory.

Section 5: Who Helps Whom?

Snapshot

People are more likely to help others who are similar to themselves, female, or beautiful. Further, people are more likely to help if they have a helpful personality and do not endorse just world beliefs.

Learning Objectives

- ❖ Describe the factors in who helps whom.
- ❖ Explain how help from friends relates to sex.

Summary

Use the appropriate terms to complete each summary.

1. In the broader public sphere, ________________________ are more likely to help, but in the family sphere, ________________________ are more likely to help. Further, we are more likely to help people who are ________________________ to us or are ________________________.

2. Just world beliefs tend to lead to ________________________, but can sometimes promote helping because people want to believe that they are good so that they can expect ________________________ things to happen to them.

Section 6: Bystander Helping in Emergencies

Snapshot

Research shows that people often fail to help when there are others around. This is called the Bystander Effect. People must complete five steps in order to provide help: notice the situation, interpret the situation, take responsibility, decide how to help, and act to help.

Learning Objectives

- ❖ Explain the five steps to helping.
- ❖ Describe the relationship between being busy and helping.

Understanding Terminology

Match the terms on the right to the definitions/examples on the left.

______ 1. The more people that are present, the less likely any one of them will help.	a. diffusion of responsibility
______ 2. Everyone present shares the responsibility, so no one takes it.	b. pluralistic ignorance
______ 3. Not helping because you fear embarrassing yourself in front of others.	c. bystander effect
______ 4. E.g., you don't seem alarmed, I guess there is no reason to be alarmed.	d. audience inhibition

Summary

Use the appropriate terms to complete each summary.

1. Kitty Genovese did not receive help even though 38 people heard her pleas. Social psychologists have found that situational factors may explain the failure of peop[le] to come to her aid. This is called the ______________________.

2. In order to provide help, people must first ______________________ that something is happening, then ______________________ the situation as an emergency, then assume personal ______________________ to help, then feel ______________________ to help, and finally overcome ______________________ to actually provide help.

Section 7: How Can We Increase Helping?

Snapshot

You are more likely to get help in a public setting if you ask a particular person to give you help in a specific way. This can overcome all of the obstacles to helping. Further, we can increase the amount of helping in general by educating people about helping, modeling helping for others, and teaching that all people are part of the larger human family.

Learning Objective

❖ Explain how helping can be increased.

Summary

Use the appropriate terms to complete each summary.

1. Research has shown that students who learn about the obstacles to helping are ______________________ helpful than students who have not heard the lecture. Further, children are more willing to be helpful if they have helping behavior ______________________ for them.

CHAPTER TEST

Multiple Choice Questions

1. Mercedes helps her neighbors paint their kitchen. When she decides to build a patio, her neighbors insist on helping. Which concept best explains this behavior?
a. cooperation
b. equality
c. the good Samaritan
d. reciprocity

2. Sarah receives a compliment from her aunt. Sarah immediately says "thank you." Sarah says thank you because there is a ___ that prescribes saying thank you after receiving a compliment.
a. law
b. norm
c. rule
d. rule of law

3. Jose works 8 hours and receives $80. Summer works 6 hours and receives $60. This represents ___
a. equity but not equality.
b. equality but not equity.
c. equity and equality.
d. neither equity or equality.

4. Which of the following conditions may reduce the tragedy of the commons?
a. when feedback on the availability of resources is given
b. when a group has a collective identity
c. when people trust one another
d. all of the above help reduce the tragedy of the commons

5. Which of the following failed, in part, because of the commons dilemma?
a. anarchy
b. communism
c. democracy
d. monarchies

6. If there is a total of $100 that can be won and two people are playing to win the money, the game is a ___
a. zero-sum game.
b. non-zero sum game.
c. commons dilemma.
d. prisoner's dilemma.

7. In Milgram's studies on obedience, it was found that ___ of people administered shocks to the maximum level, although psychiatrists predicted only ___ would go to the maximum level.
a. 90.5%; 1 in 10
b. 62.5%; 1 in 10
c. 25.5%; 1 in 100
d. 62.5%; 1 in 1000

8. If I am going to a big concert, but not sure where to park, I might just follow other cars into the lot because I think they might know something that I don't know. What is this called?
a. belief acceptance
b. normative social influence
c. information social influence
d. private conformity

9. Which of the following statements is true?
a. Research shows that the last person to order is generally the most satisfied with their choice.
b. People tend to avoid ordering the same food as others in restaurants and are happier having more variety at the table.
c. People tend to avoid ordering the same food as others in restaurants ans are less happy when they change their order.
d. Research shows that people order what they want regardless of what others at the table have ordered.

10. I see a sign that says "lost cat – reward $100." What type of help am I providing if I look for the cat because I want the $100?
a. empathy motivated
b. selfish
c. altruistic
d. egoistic

11. According to kin selection theory, which of following would be true?
a. I am more likely to help my identical twin than my non-twin sibling.
b. I am more likely to help my niece than my cousin.
c. I am more likely to help my daughter than a stranger.
d. All of the above are true.

12. Wally is in a situation where he is given an opportunity to help another student by loaning his notes. Under which condition is he most likely to provide help?
a. Wally really likes the other student.
b. Wally dislikes the other student.
c. The student is unrelated to Wally.
d. The other student needs the notes because he skipped class.

13. Nathalie is most inclined to help someone who is ___
a. beautiful.
b. low in status.
c. kind.
d. male.

4. An individual who thinks a woman deserved to get raped if she was wearing a mini-skirt likely ascribes to ___
a. altruistic helping.
b. egoistic helping.
c. the bystander effect.
d. just world beliefs.

5. If you are a Bruin fan, who are you most likely to provide help to?
a. a fan of the opponent's team after a big loss
b. a fellow Bruin
c. a male
d. none of the above

6. In a crowded concert, Pierre sprains his ankle and falls to the floor. The room is very crowded and noisy. What is the best explanation for why no one helps?
a. People are selfish and do not help unless there is a reward.
b. People were afraid of looking foolish.
c. No one noticed the situation.
d. The costs outweighed the benefits.

7. Research has found that people are more likely to help a woman who is fighting with a man if she yells, "Get away from me, I don't know you" as opposed to "Get away from me, I don't know why I ever married you." According to the text, why were people less likely to help in the second scenario?
a. People may not have interpreted it as an emergency.
b. People didn't notice the situation.
c. People experienced audience inhibition.
d. Diffusion of responsibility occurred.

8. In an emergency situation, everyone may <u>look to others for cues</u> on how to react. Yet sometimes, no one reacts. Why?
a. egoistic motives
b. diffusion of responsibility
c. audience inhibition
d. pluralistic ignorance

19. In the classic Good Samaritan study, what was the main finding?
    a. Seminary students who had just prepared a speech about the Good Samaritan were more likely to help than those who had not.
    b. Seminary students only helped if they were close to graduation and had thus learned most of the Bible's teachings.
    c. Seminary students were more likely to help only if they had time to help, regardless of the speech that was prepared.
    d. All students of the seminary helped the man in need.

20. Which of the following increases helping behavior?
    a. seeing help modeled
    b. learning about obstacles of helping
    c. appreciating that we are all on this planet together
    d. all of the above

True or False Questions

T F 1. People do not feel guilty when they receive more than they deserve.

T F 2. People are happier if they live in a society with a strong rule of law.

T F 3. Older children hoard more than younger children.

T F 4. Better relationship quality leads to forgiveness, not vice versa.

T F 5. Religious people are more likely to forgive others than non-religious people.

T F 6. The negative state relief theory seems to have more support than the empathy-altruism hypothesis.

T F 7. Men may try to help other men (who are friends) gain access to casual sex partners.

T F 8. People who believe most strongly in a just world are less likely to help the elderly.

T F 9. Feeling competent to help is an important factor in determining if people will offer help.

T F 10. Watching Barney increases helping behavior in children.

Short Essay Questions

1. What did Milgram find in his obedience studies?

2. What role does empathy play in helping behavior?

3. What are the five obstacles that can prevent people from providing help?

Suggested Readings

Campbell, W., Bush, C., Brunell, A., & Shelton, J. (2005). Understanding the social costs of narcissism: The case of the tragedy of the commons. *Personality and Social Psychology Bulletin*, *31*(10), 1358-1368.

Eek, D., & Gärling, T. (2006). Prosocials prefer equal outcomes to maximizing joint outcomes. *British Journal of Social Psychology*, *45*(2), 321-337.

Fischer, P., Greitemeyer, T., Pollozek, F., & Frey, D. (2006). The unresponsive bystander: Are bystanders more responsive in dangerous emergencies? *European Journal of Social Psychology*, *36*(2), 267-278.

Jeon, J., & Buss, D. (2006). Close relationships and costly investment: Some problems with selective investment theory. *Psychological Inquiry*, *17*(1), 45-48.

Lee, E. (2006). When and how does depersonalization increase conformity to group norms in computer-mediated communication? *Communication Research*, *33*(6), 423-447.

Answer Key

Section 1

Understanding Terminology

1.	d	6.	a
2.	j	7.	e
3.	f	8.	h
4.	g	9.	i
5.	b	10.	c

Summary

1. Prosocial, rule of law
2. reciprocity, norms, equity, equality, overbenefited, underbenefited

Section 2

Summary

1. tragedy of the commons, trust, collective

Section 3

Understanding Terminology

1.	i	7.	e
2.	b	8.	j
3.	k	9.	c
4.	d	10.	g
5.	f	11.	h
6.	a		

Summary

1. prisoner's dilemma, cooperation, competition, non-zero sum
2. forgiven
3. Milgram, obedience
4. Asch, conformed

Section 4

Understanding Terminology

1.	e	4.	f
2.	d	5.	b
3.	a	6.	c

Summary

1. egoistic helping, altruistic helping, empathy-altruism, negative state relief

Section 5

Summary

1. men, women, similar, beautiful
2. blaming the victim, good

Section 6

Understanding Terminology

1. c
2. a
3. d
4. b

Summary

1. bystander effect
2. notice, interpret, responsibility, competent, audience inhibition

Section 7

Summary

1. more, modeled

Chapter Test

Multiple Choice

1.	d	(p. 255)	11.	d	(p. 269)
2.	b	(p. 256)	12.	a	(p. 271)
3.	a	(p. 256)	13.	a	(p. 275)
4.	d	(p. 259)	14.	d	(p. 276)
5.	b	(p. 259)	15.	b	(p. 274)
6.	a	(p. 260)	16.	c	(p. 278)
7.	d	(p. 265)	17.	a	(p. 279)
8.	c	(p. 267)	18.	d	(p. 279)
9.	c	(p. 268)	19.	c	(p. 281)
10.	c	(p. 270)	20.	d	(p. 283)

True or False

1. F (p. 257)
2. T (p. 254)
3. F (p. 259)
4. F (p. 263)
5. T (p. 264)
6. F (p. 272)
7. T (p. 275)
8. T (p. 276)
9. T (p. 280)
10. T (p. 283)

Short Essay

1. What did Milgram find in his obedience studies?

    - 62.5% of participants obeyed all the way to the maximum shock level

2. What role does empathy play in helping behavior?

    - According to the empathy-altruism hypothesis, empathy is the key to altruistic helping because it motivates others to help based on reducing the other person's distress.

3. What are the five obstacles that can prevent people from providing help?

    - Noticing the situation
    - Interpreting the situation
    - Taking responsibility
    - Feeling capable or competent to help
    - Overcoming audience inhibition

CHAPTER 9 – AGGRESSION AND ANTISOCIAL BEHAVIOR

CHAPTER REVIEW

Section 1: Defining Aggression and Antisocial Behavior

Snapshot

Aggression is defined as behavior that is intended to harm a person who is motivated to avoid the harm. Aggression has been categorized into hostile and instrumental aggression and passive and active aggression. Antisocial behavior is a broader category that includes all behaviors that harm interpersonal relationships or are against cultural prescriptions.

Learning Objectives

- Explain the impact of military action on terrorism.
- Define aggression.
- Contrast hostile and instrumental aggression.
- Contrast passive aggression and active aggression.
- Explain the relation of aggression and culture.
- Describe the relation of aggression and violence.
- Define antisocial behavior and what it includes.

Understanding Terminology

Match the terms on the right to the definitions/examples on the left.

______ 1. Purposely doing something to bring harm to another person.	a. passive aggression
______ 2. Harming another person out of anger because you want them to suffer.	b. aggression
______ 3. Behavior that is harmful to interpersonal relationships or the functioning of culture.	c. violence
______ 4. Harming another person as a means to some other goal.	d. hostile aggression
______ 5. Extreme aggression.	e. antisocial behavior
______ 6. E.g., purposely not warning you about the poison in your drink.	f. instrumental aggression
______ 7. Intentionally harming someone who does not want to be harmed.	g. active aggression

Summary

Use the appropriate terms to complete each summary.

1. In order for a behavior to be aggressive, it must be ______________________ and against a person who is ______________________ to avoid harm. ______________________ aggression is usually impulsive while ______________________ aggression is usually more calculated.

2. ______________________ is aggression that causes extreme harm. ______________________ behavior is any behavior that harms interpersonal relationships or is culturally undesirable.

Section 2: Is Aggression Innate or Learned?

Snapshot

Several theories of aggression have been proposed from Freudian instinct theories, learning theories, and a combination of both instinct and learning theories.

Learning Objectives

- ❖ Describe how instinct theories and learning theories explain aggression.
- ❖ Describe whether nature, nurture, or a combination best explains aggression.

Understanding Terminology

Match the terms on the right to the definitions/examples on the left.

_____ 1. Drive for sensory and sexual satisfaction.	a. modeling
_____ 2. Drive for destruction and death.	b. thanatos
_____ 3. Learning from watching others.	c. eros

Summary

Use the appropriate terms to complete each summary.

1. ______________________ theorized that eros was the drive for life and that ______________________ was the drive for death.

2. ______________________ conducted studies in which he demonstrated that children learn aggressive behaviors by watching a ______________________.

Section 3: Inner Causes of Aggression

Snapshot

The frustration-aggression hypothesis suggests that anger stems from frustration. Subsequent theorists argued that not all aggression stems from frustration, but that other states of negative affect also produce aggression. Other variables such as age, cognitive biases, and gender are associated with aggressive behavior.

Learning Objectives

- Explain how early and more current theories described the relation of frustration and aggression.
- Describe the influence of a bad mood on aggression.
- Explain how attributions can influence aggression.
- Describe the impact of age and gender on rates of aggression.
- Contrast fight or flight with tend and befriend reactions to stress.
- Define relational aggression.
- Describe the magnitude gap present for victims and perpetrators of aggression.

Understanding Terminology

Match the terms on the right to the definitions/examples on the left.

______ 1. Frustration and aggression always co-occur.	a. frustration
______ 2. Interpreting even ambiguous situations directed toward the self as aggressive.	b. hostile expectation bias
______ 3. The victim loses more than the aggressor gains.	c. frustration-aggression hypothesis
______ 4. Expecting others to react to conflict with aggression.	d. hostile perception bias
______ 5. When something or someone prevents us from obtaining our desired goal.	e. magnitude gap
______ 6. Perceiving social interactions to be aggressive, even when they are not.	f. hostile attribution bias
______ 7. Purposefully damaging another person's social relationships.	g. tend or befriend syndrome
______ 8. Responding to stress by aggression or running away.	h. relational aggression
______ 9. Responding to stress by turning to social relationships and making friends.	i. fight or flight syndrome

Summary

Use the appropriate terms to complete each summary.

1. The ______________________-______________________ hypothesis argues that all aggressive acts stem from blocked personal goals.

2. Cognitive biases lead to aggression. Some people with a ______________________ bias interpret the ambiguous behaviors of others as being aggressive. Further, people with a ______________________ tend to interpret most social interactions as hostile.

3. Men and women respond differently to stress. Men tend to respond with ______________________, while women tend to respond with ______________________.

Section 4: Interpersonal Causes of Aggression

Snapshot

Some have argued that aggression should be examined as a form of social influence. This section also covers domestic violence, sexual violence, and displaced aggression.

Learning Objectives

- ❖ Describe how aggression can be a form of social influence.
- ❖ Define domestic violence and who the victims and perpetrators tend to be.
- ❖ Describe the rates of sexual aggression, the different outcomes for victims, and what we know about the perpetrators.
- ❖ Explain how displaced aggression operates.

Understanding Terminology

Match the terms on the right to the definitions/examples on the left.

_____ 1. E.g., I'm angry at my boss, so I hit my child because he didn't feed the cat.	a. triggered displaced aggression
_____ 2. E.g., I'm angry at my boss, so I aggress against my children.	b. domestic violence
_____ 3. Extreme aggression within the home.	c. displaced aggression

Summary

Use the appropriate terms to complete each summary.

1. ________________________ is violence that occurs between family members or people in relationships. Women between the ages of 15-44 are ________________________ likely to be injured from this violence than from muggings, car accidents, and cancer combined.

2. If you kick your dog when you are upset with someone, you are exhibiting ________________________. This is said to be ________________________ if the dog had committed some minor offense.

Section 5: External Causes of Aggression

Snapshot

The presence of weapons, the mass media, and unpleasant environments have all been implicated as causes of aggression. Further, chemicals such as testosterone, serotonin, and alcohol are all associated with aggressive behavior.

Learning Objectives

- Describe how weapons, mass media, and unpleasant environments influence aggression.
- Describe the effect of testosterone, serotonin, alcohol, and diet on aggression.

Understanding Terminology

Match the terms on the right to the definitions/examples on the left.

_____ 1. Sex hormone associated with higher levels of violence.	a. weapons effect
_____ 2. Simply having a gun in view can cause an increase in aggression.	b. testosterone
_____ 3. An important neurotransmitter in which low levels are associated with violence.	c. serotonin

Summary

Use the appropriate terms to complete each summary.

1. Research has shown that having weapons in view may encourage or promote aggressive behavior. This is called the ________________________. These cues appear to ________________________ aggressive tendencies.

2. Research has shown that higher levels of ________________________ and lower levels of ________________________ are associated with increased aggression. More than 50% of the people who committed violent crimes were ________________________ when the crimes occurred.

Section 6: Self and Culture

Snapshot

Norms and values in societies tend to curb violence and aggression. Some have theorized that most violence and aggression boils down to a lack of self-control. Although in the past it was believed that low self-esteem caused aggression, it now appears that high self-esteem that is threatened is at the root of violence. Finally, some cultures condone the use of violence in reaction to wounded pride. These are called cultures of honor.

Learning Objectives

- Explain how the norms and values of a culture may influence aggression.
- Explain how self-control and wounded pride influence aggression.
- Define culture of honor and describe how a culture of honor impacts aggression.

Understanding Terminology

Match the terms on the right to the definitions/examples on the left.

_____ 1. Losing self-respect or self-honor	a. culture of honor
_____ 2. A society that sanctions violence to protect one's honor.	b. humiliation
_____ 3. Becoming violent after having one's ego bruised.	c. running amok

Summary

Use the appropriate terms to complete each summary.

1. ______________________ is the Indonesian term for going beserk following wounded pride.

2. In a *General Theory of Crime*, the authors argued that ______________________ is the best predictor of violent crime. In the U.S. South, a ______________________ persists in which violent action as a response to threats to one's honor is accepted and justified.

Section 7: Other Antisocial Behavior

Snapshot

In addition to violence and aggression, cheating, stealing, and littering are all examples of antisocial behavior.

Learning Objectives

- ❖ Explain who cheats and what can be done to reduce cheating.
- ❖ Explain the impact of stealing and how deindividuation is involved in stealing.
- ❖ Describe how norms, both injunctive and descriptive, influence littering.

Understanding Terminology

Match the terms on the right to the definitions/examples on the left.

______ 1. A loss of self-awareness.	a. norms
______ 2. Social standards for behavior.	b. deindividuation
______ 3. Norms that help us understand what others approve of.	c. injunctive norms
______ 4. Norms that tell us what other people do.	d. descriptive norms

Summary

Use the appropriate terms to complete each summary.

1. Seventy-five percent of students admit to ________________________ in school, even though most agree that it is wrong. Seventy-five percent of employees admit ________________________ at lease once from their employer. One way to reduce littering is to create ________________________. Research has shown that ________________________ are more effective than ________________________ at reducing littering.

CHAPTER TEST

Multiple Choice Questions

1. Mary is angry that Suzy didn't invite her to her birthday party. Mary immediately calls their friend Sharon and spreads a nasty rumor about Suzy. This is an example of what type of aggression?
a. instrumental
b. violent
c. passive
d. hostile

2. Harold makes a plan to break into a rich lady's house, knock her out, and steal her jewels. This is an example of what type of aggression?
a. instrumental
b. violent
c. passive
d. hostile

3. Forcible rape would be categorized as _____
a. violence.
b. active aggression.
c. both a and b.
d. neither a or b.

4. Which of the following is the name that Freud gave to our drive for destruction and death?
a. eros
b. thanatos
c. deathtos
d. superego

5. If I watch my little brother beat up the neighbor kid and get high-fives from his friends, I am likely to learn that aggression is beneficial. This is called ____
a. modeling.
b. instinct learning.
c. aggression.
d. eros learning.

6. Under which condition are kittens most likely to become cats that kill rats?
a. if they are raised from the beginning alongside rats
b. if they are raised isolated from rats and other cats
c. if they are raised with a mother cat that kills rats
d. if they are raised watching Tom and Jerry

7. If I am on the freeway trying to get to work on time and I encounter a traffic jam, I am likely to experience ___
a. relational aggression.
b. thanatos.
c. frustration.
d. eros.

8. Mr. Nguyen always thinks that others are plotting to aggress against him. He has a ___
a. hostile expectation bias.
b. hostile attribution bias.
c. hostile perception bias.
d. tendency to relationally aggress.

9. Tomas attacks Rodrigo. According to the magnitude gap, which statement is true?
a. Tomas will gain more than Rodrigo loses.
b. Tomas will gain the same as Rodrigo loses.
c. Tomas will gain less than Rodrigo loses.
d. Rodrigo and Tomas both gain a lot.

10. According to the National Health and Social Life Survey, what percentage of women report having been forced into sexual activity against their will?
a. less than 5%
b. 5% - 15%
c. 15% - 22%
d. 22% - 33%

11. Which of the following countries has not made it illegal to spank children?
a. Israel
b. Denmark
c. Italy
d. United States

12. The "kicking the dog effect" is also called ___
a. displaced aggression.
b. animal abuse.
c. domestic violence.
d. active aggression.

13. Research has shown that the presence of a rifle and a bumper sticker that reads "vengeance" on a truck ___ the likelihood that another driver would honk at it if it didn't go when a stop light turned green.
a. decreased
b. had no effect on
c. increased

14. Research has shown that children who watch a lot of violent television are more likely to do which of the following behaviors as adults?
a. pushed, grabbed, or shoved spouse
b. threw something at a spouse
c. shoved another person
d. all of the above behaviors were higher in heavy viewers

15. Which of the following environmental factors has been found to be associated with increases aggression?
a. secondhand smoke
b. noise
c. heat
d. all of the above

16. Which of the following is not a reason why alcohol increases aggression?
a. Alcohol reduces inhibitions.
b. Alcohol decreases self-awareness.
c. Alcohol increases our defense mechanisms.
d. Alcohol disrupts executive functions.

17. Which of following characteristics is the best predictor of violence?
a. low self-esteem
b. living in poverty
c. narcissism
d. poor self-control

18. Which of the following statements is false?
a. Southern states are less supportive of wars involving U.S. troops.
b. Southern states are more accepting of corporal punishment of children.
c. Southern states have more murders per capita.
d. Southern states have fewer restrictions on gun ownership.

19. Which of the following is a good way to reduce cheating?
a. decrease self-awareness
b. increase self-awareness
c. put people into groups
d. decrease arousal

20. Under what condition are trick-or-treaters likely to steal candy?
a. when they are alone
b. when they are in big group
c. when they are anonymous and in a big group
d. when they are anonymous and alone

True or False Questions

T F 1. All aggressive acts are violent acts, but not all violent acts are aggressive.

T F 2. According to the Fruedian view, even if you received everything you wanted in life, you would still have aggressive urges.

T F 3. Family violence is the highest between siblings.

T F 4. People who experience abuse almost always become abusers themselves.

T F 5. Research has shown that giving vitamins to violent criminals reduces their level of violence.

T F 6. High levels of serotonin are associated with increased aggression.

T F 7. Humiliation may be at the heart of some terrorism and wars.

T F 8. Violence starts when self-control stops.

T F 9. Stressing descriptive norms compared to injunctive norms is more effective at curbing littering.

T F 10. People with lower academic ability are more likely to cheat than people with higher academic ability.

Short Essay Questions

1. Define aggression and compare and contrast hostile and instrumental aggression.

2. What is the relationship between frustration and aggression?

3. What is a culture of honor?

Suggested Readings

Archer, J., & Graham-Kevan, N. (2003). Do beliefs about aggression predict physical aggression to partners? *Aggressive Behavior*, *29*(1), 41-54.

Coyne, S., Archer, J., & Eslea, M. (2006). 'We're not friends anymore! unless...': The frequency and harmfulness of indirect, relational, and social aggression. *Aggressive Behavior*, *32*(4), 294-307.

Giancola, P. (2004). Executive functioning and alcohol-related aggression. *Journal of Abnormal Psychology*, *113*(4), 541-555.

Johnson, M. (2005). Domestic violence: It's not about gender--or is it? *Journal of Marriage and Family*, *67*(5), 1126-1130.

Kerr, J. (2006). Examining the Bertuzzi-Moore NHL ice hockey incident: Crossing the line between sanctioned and unsanctioned violence in sport. *Aggression and Violent Behavior*, *11*(4), 313-322.

Scharrer, E. (2005). Hypermasculinity, aggression, and television violence: An experiment. *Media Psychology*, *7*(4), 353-376.

Answer Key

Section 1

Understanding Terminology

1. g
2. d
3. e
4. f
5. c
6. a
7. b

Summary

1. intentional, motivated, hostile, instrumental
2. violence, antisocial

Section 2

Understanding Terminology

1. c
2. b
3. a

Summary

1. Freud, thanatos
2. Bandura, model

Section 3

Understanding Terminology

1. c
2. f
3. e
4. b
5. a
6. d
7. h
8. i
9. g

Summary

1. frustration, aggression
2. hostile attribution, hostile perception
3. fight or flight, tend and befriend

Section 4

Understanding Terminology

1. a
2. c
3. b

Summary

1. domestic violence, more
2. displaced aggression, triggered displaced aggression

Section 5

Understanding Terminology

1. b
2. a
3. c

Summary

1. weapons effect, increase
2. testosterone, serotonin, drinking alcohol

Section 6

Understanding Terminology

1. b
2. a
3. c

Summary

1. running amok
2. poor self control, culture of honor

Section 7

Understanding Terminology

1. b
2. a
3. c
4. d

Summary

1. cheating, stealing, antilittering norms, injunctive norms, descriptive norms

Chapter Test

Multiple Choice

1. d (p. 293)
2. a (p. 293)
3. c (p. 294)
4. b (p. 297)
5. a (p. 297)
6. c (p. 298)
7. c (p. 299)
8. b (p. 301)
9. c (p. 302)
10. c (p. 305)
11. d (p. 306)
12. a (p. 306)
13. c (p. 307)
14. d (p. 308)
15. d (p. 309)
16. c (p. 310)
17. d (p. 313)
18. a (p. 315)
19. b (p. 317)
20. c (p. 318)

True or False

1. F (p. 294)
2. T (p. 299)
3. T (p. 304)
4. F (p. 306)
5. T (p. 311)
6. F (p. 310)
7. T (p. 316)
8. T (p. 313)
9. F (p. 318)
10. F (p. 317)

Short Essay

. Define aggression and compare and contrast hostile and instrumental aggression.

- Aggression is behavior that intentionally harms another person who is motivated to avoid harm.
    - Hostile aggression is harm when harm is the end goal. Usually anger is involved.
    - Instrumental aggression is when the harm is to achieve some other goal. Something of value will be obtained as a result of the aggression. Usually the behavior is planned.

. What is the relationship between frustration and aggression?

- Early researchers proposed that frustration always resulted in aggression and that all aggression followed frustration. They called this the frustration-aggression hypothesis.
- Today, researchers agree that frustration can cause aggression, but that many other factors are also implicated in aggressive behavior.

. What is a culture of honor?

- A culture in which aggression is sanctioned and justified if it is to protect individual respect, strength, virtue.
- Describe some of the attitudes and behaviors that correlate with the acceptance of a culture of honor.

CHAPTER 10 – ATTRACTION AND EXCLUSION

CHAPTER REVIEW

Section 1: The Need to Belong

Snapshot

People have a need to belong. This need encompasses both a need for frequent contact with other people and a stable framework of ongoing relationships. People who fail to meet this need have more physical and mental health problems than people who meet this need.

Learning Objectives

- ❖ Define attraction, social acceptance and rejection (social exclusion).
- ❖ Explain why belongingness is believed to be a basic need and not just a desire.
- ❖ Describe how high levels of testosterone are a tradeoff.
- ❖ Identify the two parts of the need to belong.
- ❖ Describe the effect of not belonging.

Understanding Terminology

Match the terms on the right to the definitions/examples on the left.

______ 1. A desire to be close to another person.	a. rejection
______ 2. We all hope we never have to experience this.	b. social acceptance
______ 3. We all strive for this.	c. need to belong
______ 4. A desire to be a part of relationships or groups.	d. attraction

Summary

Use the appropriate terms to complete each summary.

1. If you find yourself being drawn toward another person, you are feeling an ________________ for that person. As social beings we strive for ________________ and desire to avoid ________________. This is related to our ıeed to ________________.

2. The hormone ________________ has been shown to be better suited for ________________ mates as opposed to ________________ relationships. As he text points out, there are many ________________ associated with this hormone. For example, men with high ________________ are more likely to perform ________________ and more likely to commit ________________.

Section 2: Attraction: Who Likes Whom?

Snapshot

Research has shown that we tend to be attracted to people who are rewarding to us in some way. People who are similar to us, people who like us in return, people who are near us, and people who are beautiful are all rewarding to us.

Learning Objectives

- ❖ Define ingratiation.
- ❖ Explain the role of similarity in liking.
- ❖ Define self-monitoring.
- ❖ Explain the matching hypothesis.
- ❖ Explain how reinforcement theory, reciprocation, propinquity and mere exposure, and attractiveness help explain who we like.
- ❖ Describe the social allergy effect.
- ❖ Explain the role of propinquity in who our friends and our enemies are.
- ❖ Describe the what is beautiful is good effect.
- ❖ Explain how symmetry and typicality relates to beauty.

Understanding Terminology

Match the terms on the right to the definitions/examples on the left.

______ 1. Being in close proximity often.	a. self-monitoring
______ 2. We will repeat behaviors that were previously rewarded.	b. social allergy effect
______ 3. I am attempting this if I am trying to get you to like me.	c. reinforcement theory
______ 4. Friends and lovers tend to be equally attractive.	d. propinquity
______ 5. Believing that beautiful people also have other positive qualities.	e. ingratiation
______ 6. Changing behavior to fit a particular social environment.	f. what is beautiful is good effect
______ 7. Things you don't like initially become even more irritating over time.	g. matching hypothesis

Summary

Use the appropriate terms to complete each summary.

1. As social creatures, we spend a lot of time working to get others to like us. This is called ___________________.

2. Researchers have identified a number of important variables that are associated with attraction. For example, research has found that we are attracted to others who are ___________________ to us. When this is in the realm of physical attractiveness, we call it the ___________________ hypothesis. We also like people who ___________________ our liking. In other words, liking begets liking. Finally, we may find ourselves being attracted to someone who lives next door to us or who works in the office next to ours. This ___________________ effect is very powerful.

3. Finally, we may be attracted to beautiful people because of the ___________________ effect. We tend to think beautiful people are also happy, warm, and intelligent.

Section 3: Rejection

Snapshot

Being rejected by others is a powerful psychological experience that can lead to inner reactions such as developing rejection sensitivity and behavioral reactions including being less generous and more aggressive. A related idea is loneliness. Loneliness occurs when a person's social interaction needs are not met. This is usually about the quality of interactions, but can be from too few interactions. Finally, this chapter will discuss why people reject others and the experience of unrequited love.

Learning Objectives

- Define ostracism and describe its effect.
- Explain the internal reactions individuals have to rejection, including rejection sensitivity, numbness and eating behaviors.
- Describe how people respond to rejection behaviorally.
- Define loneliness and describe who is lonely.
- Explain the causes of rejection by children and adults.
- Define the bad apple effect and how it relates to rejection.
- Explain the experience of unrequited love and its effect.

Understanding Terminology

Match the terms on the right to the definitions/examples on the left.

_____ 1. A personality trait in which the person comes to expect rejection.	a. ostracism
_____ 2. Unreciprocated attraction.	b. bad apple effect
_____ 3. A feeling that is experienced when your need for social interactions is unmet.	c. stalking
_____ 4. Persistent attempts at forming a relationship when unwanted.	d. rejection sensitivity
_____ 5. Having others reject or exclude you from social interaction.	e. unrequited love
_____ 6. Concern that if one person violates the norms, that others will follow suit.	f. loneliness

Summary

Use the appropriate terms to complete each summary.

1. One form of rejection is __________________ in which people ignore your presence. The word originates from ancient __________________. People who expect others to hurt their feelings and thus often push others away are said to possess a personality trait called __________________.

2. People may experience a painful feeling called __________________ when their social needs are not met. Generally, in today's modern world, loneliness stems from __________________ interactions as opposed to a low __________________ of interactions.

3. People reject others for a whole host of reasons. Research has found three main reasons that children reject other children. First, children reject __________________ children because they are un-liked and considered dangerous. Children also reject those who have __________________ from social contact, thus creating a vicious circle. Finally, children also reject __________________ children. In other words, children reject children who are different from the norm in some way.

CHAPTER TEST

Multiple Choice Questions

1. Big is to little as social acceptance is to ___
   a. friendship.
   b. rejection.
   c. the need to belong.
   d. attraction.

2. Which statement best summarizes Warren Jones' research findings on loneliness?
   a. About 10% of people prefer to be loners.
   b. Many people have no friends, but say they are happy that way.
   c. Many people say they have no friends, but everyone desires to have friends.
   d. Loneliness is an unimportant variable as it is not associated with well-being.

Which of the following statements is true about the hormone testosterone?
a. After the age of about 20, levels of testosterone decline in men.
b. After the birth of their child, men's testosterone level drops.
c. High testosterone is associated with greater violence.
d. All of the above are true.

How is the "need to belong" associated with larger and smarter brains?
a. Our brains evolved to be larger and smarter to keep track of social connections.
b. Once we had larger social networks, the brain that we had originally developed to hunt and gather food was commandeered to help keep track of our social lives.
c. Very little of our brain is used to keep track of our social lives.
d. None of the above are true.

What are the two ingredients of belongingness?
a. regular social contact and a supportive caregiver
b. a supportive caregiver and a stable framework of on-going relationships
c. regular social contact and a stable framework of on-going relationships
d. love and kindness

Most people think that having between _____ friends is a sufficient.
a. 2 – 5
b. 4 – 6
c. 6 – 8
d. 8 – 10

If Martina lives in apartment 5 in a building with along hallway in which the apartments are numbered from 1 -15, based on the ___ effect, she is likely to be attracted to the people in apartment 4 and 6.
a. propinquity
b. what is beautiful is good
c. similarity
d. reciprocity

Carol finds that when she is with her friends, she is very outspoken and lively, but when she is with her grandparents she is very quiet and reserved. Based on this description, she is likely to be a(n) ___
a. introvert.
b. extrovert.
c. high social monitor.
d. low social monitor.

9. Which of the following is true about the matching hypothesis?
   a. It is found among same-sex and opposite sex romantic partners.
   b. It is found among friend pairs as well as romantic partners.
   c. It states that people pair up with people of similar attractiveness level.
   d. All of the above are true.

10. What are the two broad strategies that are usually successful in getting others to like you based on reinforcement theory?
   a. doing favors and making promises
   b. doing favors and giving praise
   c. giving praise and providing reassurance
   d. providing reassurance and giving money

11. Becoming more annoyed with people's habits over time is called ___
   a. the propinquity effect.
   b. the buffering hypothesis.
   c. the social allergy effect.
   d. the 'I can't stand it anymore' effect.

12. Which of the following is not generally regarded as beautiful?
   a. symmetry
   b. uniqueness
   c. clear complexion
   d. typicality

13. Which of the following is not true about preferences for attractive people?
   a. Attractive children are more popular than their peers.
   b. Three-month-old babies prefer looking at attractive faces.
   c. People are quicker to be violent against attractive faces.
   d. Good looking people do better in job interviews.

14. Where does the word ostracism orginate?
   a. Rome
   b. Greece
   c. South Africa
   d. Iceland

15. What personality trait does a person who expects rejection and thus avoids getting close to others have?
   a. self-devaluation
   b. neuroticism
   c. loneliness
   d. rejection sensitivity

6. Which of the following concepts explain why people eat more junk food after experiencing social rejection?
   a. self-control
   b. self-esteem
   c. evolved hunger response
   d. avoidance

7. Which of the following is not true about recently rejected individuals?
   a. They are less helpful toward others.
   b. They are more willing to cheat or break rules.
   c. They are more compassionate toward others.
   d. They show decreases in intelligent thought.

8. Which of the following statements is true?
   a. Nonlonely people spend more time with other people compared to lonely people.
   b. Nonlonely people tend to be more intelligent than lonely people.
   c. Nonlonely people tend to be more attractive than lonely people.
   d. There are very few differences between lonely and nonlonely people.

9. Which behavior would result in the most negative evaluation?
   a. bad behavior by someone in your own social group
   b. bad behavior by someone in a different social group
   c. no difference in the negative evaluation

10. Using the dimensions of attribution theory, if Helena rejected Kevin for a date, her private reasons were ___ while the reasons she told Kevin were ___.
   a. internal, stable and global; external, unstable, specific
   b. external, unstable, specific; internal, stable and global
   c. internal, unstable, and global; external, stable, specific
   d. external; stable, specific; external, stable, global

True or False Questions

T F 1. Inmates in solitary confinement accept their solitary punishment and do not attempt to communicate with others.

T F 2. Loneliness can impair our immune system and make it more difficult to recuperate from sickness or injury.

T F 3. Testosterone helps men find mates but may not be helpful in maintaining stable families.

T F 4. The scarcity and availability of food influences ideal body weight.

T F 5. Averaging faces results in more beautiful faces, but only when averaging up to eight faces.

T F 6. "Opposites attract" is often true.

T F 7. Having someone mimic our non-verbal behaviors is associated with a greater liking for that person.

T F 8. Women are more likely to stalk others than men.

T F 9. People who are ostracized may experience problems including pain, helplessness, and suicidal thoughts.

T F 10. Men are more likely than women to stave off loneliness through connections to large groups or organizations.

Short Essay Questions

1. Describe the two ingredients of the need to belong. Is it possible to experience one and not the other?

2. Name and describe four important variables that are associated with attraction.

3. What do hurt feelings have to do with rejection?

uggested Readings

arvallo, M., & Gabriel, S. (2006). No man is an island: The need to belong and dismissing avoidant attachment style. *Personality and Social Psychology Bulletin, 32*(5), 697-709.

arvallo, M., & Pelham, B. (2006). When fiends become friends: The need to belong and perceptions of personal and group discrimination. *Journal of Personality and Social Psychology, 90*(1), 94-108.

isenberger, N., Lieberman, M., & Williams, K. (2003). Does rejection hurt? An fMRI study of social exclusion. *Science, 302*(5643), 290-292.

ehr, A., & Geher, G. (2006). Differential effects of reciprocity and attitude similarity across long- versus short-term mating contexts. *Journal of Social Psychology, 146*(4), 423-439.

hillips, L., Quirk, R., Rosenfeld, B., & O'Connor, M. (2004). Is it stalking? Perceptions of stalking among college undergraduates. *Criminal Justice and Behavior, 31*(1), 73-96.

aidel, D., Aarde, S., & Baig, K. (2005). Appearance of symmetry, beauty, and health in human faces. *Brain and Cognition, 57*(3), 261-263.

nswer Key

ection 1

Understanding Terminology

1. d
2. a
3. b
4. c

Summary

1. attraction, social acceptance, rejection, belong
2. testosterone, attracting, maintaining, tradeoffs, testosterone, heroic acts, imes

Section 2

Understanding Terminology

1. d
2. c
3. e
4. g
5. f
6. a
7. b

Summary

1. ingratiation
2. similar, matching, reciprocate, propinquity
3. what is beautiful is good

Section 3

Understanding Terminology

1. d
2. e
3. f
4. c
5. a
6. b

Summary

1. ostracism, Greece, rejection sensitivity
2. loneliness, poor quality, quantity
3. aggressive, withdrawn, deviant

Chapter Test

Multiple Choice

1.	b	(p. 327)	11.	c	(p. 337)
2.	c	(p. 327)	12.	b	(p. 340)
3.	d	(p. 328)	13.	c	(p. 339)
4.	a	(p. 330)	14.	b	(p. 342)
5.	c	(p. 331)	15.	d	(p. 343)
6.	b	(p. 331)	16.	a	(p. 344)
7.	a	(p. 337)	17.	c	(p. 345)
8.	d	(p. 333)	18.	d	(p. 346)
9.	d	(p. 334)	19.	a	(p. 348)
10.	b	(p. 335)	20.	a	(p. 349)

True or False

1. F (p. 329)
2. T (p. 332)
3. T (p. 328)
4. T (p. 339)
5. F (p. 340)
6. F (p. 333)
7. T (p. 336)
8. F (p. 350)
9. T (p. 342)
10. T (p. 347)

Short Essay

1. Describe the two ingredients of the need to belong. Is it possible to experience one and not the other?

- Regular social contacts – doing positive or neutral things with other individuals.
- Stable framework of ongoing relationships – the framework provides knowledge that there are people who will consistently be there with whom you share mutual concern for each other.
- Yes, it is possible to have one and not the other. A person may have a lot of social contact but no framework, or a person's framework may consist of people who live at a distance and thus not have regular social contact.

2. Name and describe four important variables that are associated with attraction.

- Similarity – we like people who are similar to us
- Reciprocity – we like people who like us
- Propinquity – we like people who are near us (due to familiarity)
- Physical beauty – we like attractive people (what is good is beautiful effect)

3. What do hurt feelings have to do with rejection?

- Often, hurt feelings occur because a behavior (or lack of behavior) implied that the person does not care about your relationship with him or her. This then implies rejection! It may not be intentional, but may be interpreted as rejection.

CHAPTER 11 – CLOSE RELATIONSHIPS: PASSION, INTIMACY, AND SEXUALITY

CHAPTER REVIEW

Section 1: What Is Love?

Snapshot

Two major types of love include passionate love (often the pull to begin new relationships) and companionate love (more important to long-lasting relationships). Further, Sternberg theorized that love consists of three different ingredients: passion, intimacy, and commitment. Different relationships have differing amounts of these three ingredients.

Learning Objectives

- ❖ Compare and contrast passionate love (romantic love) and companionate love (affectionate love).
- ❖ Describe how passionate love is understood across cultures.
- ❖ Explain the course of passionate love and companionate love over the duration of a relationship.
- ❖ Describe the relationship of marriage, singlehood, and sex.
- ❖ Explain Sternberg's triangle theory of love.

Understanding Terminology

Match the terms on the right to the definitions/examples on the left.

_____ 1. Sternberg's ingredient that is characterized by closeness and concern.	a. commitment
_____ 2. Love characterized by friendship and mutual support and caring.	b. intimacy
_____ 3. Sternberg's ingredient that is characterized by the decision to stay.	c. passion
_____ 4. Sternberg's ingredient that is characterized by bodily arousal.	d. companionate love
_____ 5. Love characterized by strong feeling of desire and longing.	e. passionate love

Summary

Use the appropriate terms to complete each summary.

1. Two main types of love have been distinguished. The first is ______________________, characterized by strong emotions and desire. The second is ______________________ , characterized by being "best friends." ______________________ is more important to the longevity of romantic relationships.

2. Sternberg's triangular theory of love consists of ______________________, ______________________, and ______________________.

Section 2: Different Types of Relationships

Snapshot

Exchange relationships are based on reciprocity and fairness while communal relationships are based on mutual love and concern. Many people strive for communal relationships at home and exchange relationships at work. Attachment is another important concept to understanding relationships. Attachment styles explain people's approach to and expectations of close relationships. The evolution of attachment theory is discussed in this section.

Learning Objectives

- Compare exchange relationships with communal relationships.
- Describe the original three types of attachments and the later 4 types of attachment.
- Describe how attachment style affects relationships and sex.
- Explain the effect of self-esteem, narcissism, and self-acceptance on relationships.

Understanding Terminology

Match the terms on the right to the definitions/examples on the left.

_____ 1. An attachment style characterized by wanting to be close but worrying about being abandoned.	a. attachment theory
_____ 2. E.g., no need to keep track of what we've done for one another.	b. fearful avoidant attachment
_____ 3. Thinking of oneself as a good person.	c. exchange relationships
_____ 4. A theory of different approaches to close relationships.	d. preoccupied attachment
_____ 5. An attachment style characterized by trusting one's partner and enjoying the relationship.	e. dismissing avoidant attachment
_____ 6. E.g., if I give you something, I'll expect something in return.	f. self-acceptance
_____ 7. An attachment style characterized by devaluing the self and keeping others at a distance.	g. communal relationships
_____ 8. An attachment style characterized by viewing partners as unreliable.	h. secure attachment

Summary

Use the appropriate terms to complete each summary.

1. Keeping separate bank accounts and tracking whose turn it is to do the dishes is ndicative of a(n) ______________________ relationship. ______________________ elationships are characterized by mutual concern and support without expectation of epayment.

2. The two main dimensions of attachment are ______________________ and ______________________. People with ______________________ attachment tend o have more durable and satisfying relationship compared to the other three ategories.

Section 3: Maintaining Relationships

Snapshot

Maintaining relationships over the long haul can be challenging. Many couples fail, but many others find success. Rusbult's investment model theorized that commitment is high when there is high satisfaction, high investments, and low quality of alternatives. Other research suggests that the way the people think abou their romantic partners is important to relationship maintenance. Finally, the role of honesty in relationships will be discussed.

Learning Objectives

- ❖ Describe whether relationships improve over time, both in people's judgments and in reality.
- ❖ Explain the investment model.
- ❖ Describe the impact of positive and negative interactions on relationships, including the impact of the reciprocity of negative behavior.
- ❖ Describe the difference between a relationship-enhancing style of attribution anc a distress-maintaining style of attribution.
- ❖ Explain the impact on a relationship across time of seeing a relationship partner as they see themselves versus idealizing a relationship partner.

Understanding Terminology

Match the terms on the right to the definitions/examples on the left.

_____ 1. E.g., you hurt me, so I hurt you.

_____ 2. Model using three components to predict commitment.

_____ 3. E.g., you must be late for dinner because you are irresponsible.

_____ 4. E.g., you must be late for dinner because of terrible traffic.

a. relationship-enhancing style of attribution

b. investment model

c. reciprocity of negative behavior

d. distress-maintaining style

Summary

Use the appropriate terms to complete each summary.

1. Rusbult's model contains three predictors of commitment. As the ______________________ (things put into the relationship that cannot be retrieved) go up, commitment goes up. As ______________________ (the benefits of the relationship) goes up, commitment goes up. As ______________________ (availability and assessment of other partners) goes up, commitment goes down.

2. If Wanda assumes that her husband brought her flowers because he is a warm and caring man, she is making a ______________________ attribution. However, if Wanda assumes that her husband brought her flowers because they were on sale, she is making a ______________________ attribution.

Section 4: Sexuality

Snapshot

Researchers have examined several different dimensions of sexuality. This section discusses how love and sex may be discreet systems. Other researchers have examined the similarities and differences in the sexuality of men and women. Jealousy and extradyadic sex are also discussed.

Learning Objectives

- Explain the two separate systems of attachment and the sex drive.
- Compare and contrast the social constructionist theories, evolutionary theory an social exchange theory explanations of sexual behavior, including what research support has been found for each.
- Describe whether there is any accuracy in the stereotypes that men want more sex than women, men separate love and sex more than women, that women's sexuality is more natural, men's is based more in culture, and that women serve as gatekeepers for sex (restrict sex in a relationship).
- Define the Coolidge effect and erotic plasticity.
- Describe the effect the presence an attractive member of the opposite sex has on the eating behavior of men and women.
- Explain why homosexuality is a puzzle and Bem's explanation for its development.
- Describe the rate of extradyadic sex in U.S. culture, attitudes toward it, its effect on the course of a relationship, and the reasons individuals give for engaging in extradyadic sex.
- Explain the cultural and evolutionary perspectives on jealousy and possessiveness.
- Describe the causes of jealousy and whether individuals are accurate about thei jealous beliefs.
- Describe whether there is a double standard for men or women in western culture.

Understanding Terminology

Match the terms on the right to the definitions/examples on the left.

______ 1. Whether social, cultural, and situational forces change a person's sex drive.	a. Coolidge effect
______ 2. Sex with a person other than one's own partner.	b. paternity uncertainty
______ 3. Theorizes that our sexual preferences have been shaped by natural selection.	c. social constructionist theories
______ 4. When women receive more scorn than men for the same behavior.	d. double standard
______ 5. New partners are quickly arousing.	e. extradyadic sex
______ 6. Beliefs shared by many people.	f. social exchange theory
______ 7. "Mama's baby, daddy's maybe."	g. reverse double standard
______ 8. Theories that suggest that our attitudes and behaviors are shaped by culture.	h. social reality
______ 9. When men receive more scorn than women for the same behavior.	i. evolutionary theory
______ 10. Theorizes that our behavior is based on weighing benefits and costs.	j. erotic plasticity

Summary

Use the appropriate terms to complete each summary.

1. Researchers who believe that culture and society shape our sexual attitudes and desires call themselves ______________________. On the other hand, researchers who believe that our sexuality was shaped by millions of years of natural selection call themselves ______________________.

2. Research has shown that women demonstrate ______________________ erotic plasticity than men. Research has also shown that women tend to be the ______________________ of sex. In other words, women often dictate when a couple has sex and how long they wait before having sex.

3. People generally report having very ______________________ attitudes toward extradyadic sex. Further, only ______________________ of men and ______________________ of women report having ever engaged in extradyadic sex.

CHAPTER TEST

Multiple Choice Questions

1. Jim and Chris began dating a few weeks ago. They cannot seem to get enough of one another. They constantly want to be together and light up when the other enters the room. What type of love are they most likely experiencing?
   a. affectionate
   b. passionate
   c. companionate
   d. committed

2. What type of love is exemplified by saying, "My husband is my best friend?"
   a. companionate
   b. passionate
   c. free
   d. friendship

3. Which of the following is not one of Sternberg's three ingredients of love?
   a. intimacy
   b. passion
   c. attachment
   d. commitment

4. Which biochemical is associated with passionate love?
   a. phenylethylamine
   b. testosterone
   c. serotonin
   d. progesterone

5. Two people who have been married for 30 years who "stayed together for the sake of the kids" are likely to be highest in which of Sternberg's three ingredients?
   a. intimacy
   b. passion
   c. attachment
   d. commitment

6. What type of relationship do people usually have with their neighborhood grocery clerk?
   a. communal
   b. companionate
   c. exchange
   d. avoidant

7. Long term love relationships are typically ____ relationships.
   a. communal
   b. passionate
   c. exchange
   d. avoidant

8. Juanita desires to be close to other people but worries that others might abandon her. What attachment style does this exemplify?
   a. secure
   b. fearful avoidant
   c. dismissing avoidant
   d. preoccupied

9. In which attachment style are people often seen as withdrawn or aloof?
   a. secure
   b. fearful avoidant
   c. dismissing avoidant
   d. preoccupied

10. In which attachment style are people worried that they are unlovable even as they think others are untrustworthy?
    a. secure
    b. fearful avoidant
    c. dismissing avoidant
    d. preoccupied

11. According to Gottman's research, how many positive interactions are needed to offset the impact of one negative interaction?
    a. 1
    b. 2
    c. 5
    d. 9

12. What is it called when partner A says something nasty to partner B and then partner B responds with something nasty?
    a. distress maintaining attribution
    b. reciprocity of negative behavior
    c. downward spiral of negativity
    d. social constructionist view of relationships

13. According to Rusbult's model, what would time spent building a relationship be considered?
a. satisfaction
b. investments
c. emotional connectivity
d. quality of alternatives

14. What characterizes a relationship-enhancing attribution style?
a. explain good behavior with internal factors
b. explain bad behavior with internal factors
c. explain bad behavior with external factors
d. a and c

15. Which of the following statements best characterizes the research findings on whether it is good to see a partner honestly or in an idealized manner?
a. Seeing the true partner is always best.
b. Idealizing a partner is beneficial for relationship success.
c. It is good to see a partner honestly in the little things, but in a more general sense to idealize a partner.
d. It is good to idealize a partner about trivial things, but you must see the true partner when it comes to generalizations.

16. The idea that women's sexuality is a valuable resource that men want describes the ___ of sexuality.
a. social constructionist theory
b. evolutionary theory
c. social exchange theory
d. feminist theory

17. Which of the following statements is evidence that women have greater erotic plasticity than men?
a. Women go through many changes in their sexual feelings and desires.
b. Education has a greater effect on women's sexuality than men's.
c. Religion has a greater effect on women's sexuality than men's.
d. All of the above are evidence of greater erotic plasticity in women.

18. According to self-report data, what percentage of married women have extradyadic sex?
a. less than 5%
b. about 10%
c. about 25%
d. about 50%

19. What statement summarizes the general finding regarding the double standard?
    a. People tend to judge women harsher than men when it comes to having premarital sex.
    b. Men apply the double standard more readily than women.
    c. Women apply the reverse double standard.
    d. Support for the double standard is weak and when found, it is usually women supporting it.

20. What is the Coolidge effect?
    a. having multiple sex partners as President Coolidge preferred
    b. the finding that people tend to be cool at first to new partners, but overtime warm up
    c. the power that new partners have in being arousing compared to familiar partners
    d. none of the above

True or False Questions

T F 1. The decline in sex among married couples is completely due to the aging process.

T F 2. In the past year, single people are more likely to have multiple sexual partners and more likely to have no sexual partners compared to married people.

T F 3. Women with a preoccupied attachment style are more likely to have sex with partners even when they do not want to do so.

T F 4. People who love themselves (a lot) make the best relationship partners.

T F 5. People tend to fall in love with an idealized version of a person.

T F 6. A distress-maintaining style of attribution is particularly harmful because even positive behaviors get discounted.

T F 7. Each factor in Rusbult's model is weakly associated with whether couples stay or leave a relationship.

T F 8. Women eat less when they are with attractive available men.

T F 9. Research has found that people think their own infidelities are less excusable than their partner's infidelities.

T F 10. Men may have extradyadic sex even when they have no complaints about their marriage.

Short Essay Questions

1. Describe Sternberg's triangular theory of love.

2. Provide examples of how people may explain positive and negative behaviors depending on attribution styles. How does this relate to relationship maintenance?

3. How does Lisa Diamond's work explain falling in love with someone of the "wrong" gender?

Suggested Readings

Kito, M. (2005). Self-disclosure in romantic relationships and friendships among American and Japanese college students. *Journal of Social Psychology*, *145*(2), 127-140.

Foster, J., & Campbell, W. (2005). Narcissism and resistance to doubts about romantic partners. *Journal of Research in Personality*, *39*(5), 550-557.

Sprecher, S. (1999). 'I love you more today than yesterday': Romantic partners' perceptions of changes in love and related affect over time. *Journal of Personality and Social Psychology*, *76*(1), 46-53.

Diamond, L. (2004). Emerging perspectives on distinctions between romantic love and sexual desire. *Current Directions in Psychological Science*, *13*(3), 116-119.

Diamond, L. (2005). 'I'm straight, but I kissed a girl': The trouble with American media representations of female-female sexuality. *Feminism & Psychology*, *15*(1), 104-110.

Buunk, B., & Bakker, A. (1995). Extradyadic sex: The role of descriptive and injunctive norms. *Journal of Sex Research*, *32*(4), 313-318.

Answer Key

Section 1

Understanding Terminology

1. b
2. d
3. a
4. c
5. e

Summary

1. passionate love, companionate love, companionate love
2. passion, intimacy, commitment

Section 2

Understanding Terminology

1. d	5. h
2. g	6. c
3. f	7. b
4. a	8. e

Summary

1. exchange, communal
2. anxiety, avoidance, secure

Section 3

Understanding Terminology

1. c
2. b
3. d
4. a

Summary

1. investments, satisfaction, quality of alternatives
2. relationship-enhancing, distress-maintaining

Section 4

Understanding Terminology

1. j	6. h
2. e	7. b
3. i	8. c
4. d	9. g
5. a	10. f

Summary

1. social constructionists, evolutionary theorists
2. more, gatekeepers
3. negative, 23%, 12%

Chapter Test

Multiple Choice

1.	b	(p. 360)	11.	c	(p. 373)
2.	a	(p. 360)	12.	b	(p. 373)
3.	c	(p. 364)	13.	b	(p. 374)
4.	a	(p. 361)	14.	d	(p. 375)
5.	d	(p. 364)	15.	c	(p. 377)
6.	c	(p. 365)	16.	c	(p. 380)
7.	a	(p. 366)	17.	d	(p. 383)
8.	d	(p. 368)	18.	b	(p. 386)
9.	c	(p. 369)	19.	d	(p. 394)
10.	b	(p. 369)	20.	c	(p. 382)

True or False

1.	F	(p. 362)
2.	T	(p. 363)
3.	T	(p. 369)
4.	F	(p. 370)
5.	T	(p. 376)
6.	T	(p. 375)
7.	T	(p. 374)
8.	T	(p. 384)
9.	F	(p. 388)
10.	T	(p. 389)

Short Essay

1. Describe Sternberg's triangular theory of love.

   - The triangle is made up of three sides consisting of passion, intimacy, and commitment.
   - Any love relationship can consist of varying degrees of these three ingredients. All combinations are possible.

2. Provide examples of how people may explain positive and negative behaviors depending on attribution styles. How does this relate to relationship maintenance?
   - Relationship-enhancing attributions are when people attribute good behavior to internal causes (e.g. you brought me flowers because you are thoughtful) and negative behavior to external causes (e.g. you shouted at me because your day at work was so stressful). This pattern helps relationships stay positive.
   - Distress-maintaining attributions are when people attribute good behavior to external causes (e.g. you brought me flowers because they were on sale) and negative behaviors to internal causes (e.g. you shouted at me because you are mean). As the name suggests, these attributions create and maintain distress in the relationships as even good behaviors do not get reflected positively on the partner.

3. How does Lisa Diamond's work explain falling in love with someone of the "wrong" gender?
   - Diamond theorizes that intimacy and sexual attraction evolved separately from one another. She argues that intimacy is gender neutral allowing both men and women to have close, caring relationships with men and women. This is the attachment system and promoted closeness. On the other hand, sexual desire evolved to be directed toward people of the opposite sex to promote procreation. This can cause "problems" when humans mix intimacy with sex. Humans often become sexually attracted to people with whom they share intimacy and vice versa.

CHAPTER 12 – PREJUDICE AND INTERGROUP RELATIONS

CHAPTER REVIEW

Section 1: Common Prejudices and Targets

Snapshot

The ABCs of negative intergroup relations consist of Affect (prejudice), Behavior (Discrimination), and Cognition (Stereotype). In order to simplify the world, our mind puts things (including people) into categories. Placing people into groups is called social categorization. This categorization sets up in-group and out-group distinctions. This section reviews prejudice against Arabs, gay men and lesbians, and overweight people.

Learning Objectives

- Define prejudice, racism, aversive racism, discrimination, and stereotypes.
- Understand how subtypes, social categorization, and ingroup, outgroup, and outgroup homogeneity bias relate to stereotypes.
- Understand prejudice as it relates to Arabs, people who are overweight, and homosexuals.
- Define stigma and stigma by association.

Understanding Terminology

Match the terms on the right to the definitions/examples on the left.

_____ 1. Unfair behavior directed at a person because of group membership.	a. racism
_____ 2. People who do not belong to my social group.	b. social categorization
_____ 3. Negative affect toward a person because of group membership.	c. outgroup homogeneity bias
_____ 4. The forming of these make stereotypes resistant to change.	d. aversive racism
_____ 5. "They are all alike; we are all different."	e. ingroup members
_____ 6. Being connected to a stigmatized person can result in stigmatization.	f. subtypes
_____ 7. Prejudice directed at a group of people based on their race.	g. homophobia
_____ 8. People who belong to my same social group.	h. discrimination
_____ 9. Attributes of a person that bring devaluation or scorn.	i. categorization
_____ 10. The automatic separating of objects into groups.	j. prejudice
_____ 11. Fear of gays and lesbians.	k. stigmas
_____ 12. Believing in racial equality while simultaneously holding negative feelings.	l. outgroup members
_____ 13. Separating people into groups based on common characteristics.	m. stereotypes
_____ 14. Characteristics assigned to a person because of social group membership.	n. stigma by association

Summary

Use the appropriate terms to complete each summary.

1. People have a tendency to ________________________ others into groups. You are a(n) ________________________ member with those you share membership and others are ________________________ members. You may find that you have negative affect for those that are different; this is called ________________________. If you think that all the others are likely to have the same attribute, you are applying a ________________________. And if you behave unfairly toward a person in the other group, you are enacting ________________________.

2. Research has found that people can be stigmatized by just being around someone who belongs to a devalued group; this is called ________________________. Three groups that are stigmatized, without apology, in our society include ________________________, ________________________, and ________________________.

Section 2: Why Prejudice Exists

Snapshot

A number of different theories have been put forth to explain prejudice. Competition for scarce resources, ignorance, rationalization for oppression, simplification of the world using stereotypes, and boosts to self-esteem have all been used to explain why prejudice exists. Each of these ideas is discussed in this section.

Learning Objectives

- Explain how ingroup favoritism and minimal group effect help explain prejudice and stereotypes.
- Explain how cooperation and competition among groups are related to prejudice and stereotyping, including the effect of realistic group conflict theory and superordinate goals.
- Explain the contact hypothesis and the issues with it.
- Describe how rationalization for oppression, heuristics, and self-esteem are related to prejudice.

Understanding Terminology

Match the terms on the right to the definitions/examples on the left.

______ 1. Treating members of one's own group better than members of the outgroup.	a. realistic conflict theory
______ 2. When only one group can win.	b. minimal group effect
______ 3. These require everyone's cooperation for success to be obtained.	c. cooperation
______ 4. When people work together on common goals.	d. discontinuity effect
______ 5. Ingroup favoritism will occur even when groups are based on arbitrary divisions.	e. superordinate goals
______ 6. You and I might be able to get along, but our groups will not.	f. competition
______ 7. Competition for scarce commodities leads to ingroup and outgroup biases.	g. contact hypothesis
______ 8. With knowledge of the other group through interaction, prejudice will be diminished.	h. ingroup favoritism

Summary

Use the appropriate terms to complete each summary.

1. Having more favorable attitudes toward one's own group is called ________________________. This occurs even if groups are made on some arbitrary dimension and is known as the ________________________.

2. Two groups of boys, age 11, developed negative attitudes toward one another after ________________________ for prizes. This can be explained by ________________________ theory. Only after working to achieve ________________________ goals with ________________________ did the boys become friends.

3. Researchers have suggested that one reason for prejudice is a lack of knowledge of other people and other groups. The proposed remedy was ________________________. However, it was found that this hypothesis only worked if three important conditions were met. These included ________________________, interactions that were ________________________, and a belief that outgroup members were ________________________ of their group.

Section 3: Content of Prejudice and Stereotypes

Snapshot

Although stereotypes are dangerous and usually exaggerated, some research has found that at the root of stereotypes may be "kernals of truth." If stereotypes serve as heuristics, they should be accurate more often than not to provide any useful purpose. However, when stereotypes exist to maintain the status quo or to oppress an entire group of people, they may be terribly exaggerated or completely false. Research has also shown that negative stereotypes are much more resistant to change and this may explain why more negative stereotypes exist than positive stereotypes.

Learning Objectives

- Explain if stereotypes are always completely wrong or always negative.

Summary

Use the appropriate terms to complete each summary.

1. Some researchers think that stereotypes may have a ________________________, even though they are generally exaggerated. Other research shows that it is more difficult to change ________________________ stereotypes compared to ________________________ stereotypes.

Section 4: Inner Processes

Snapshot

Prejudice may arise from inner processes. For example, we may develop biases from things that are salient around us. Or we may develop biases as a way to blame outgroup members for our own failures. Finally, our assumptions or our tendency to confirm our existing beliefs may lead to prejudice and stereotypic thinking.

Learning Objectives

- Describe the inner processes of salience, scapegoat theory, and assumptions in relation to prejudice.

Understanding Terminology

Match the terms on the right to the definitions/examples on the left.

_____ 1. Holding prejudice against an outgroup because you blame them for problems.	a. salience
_____ 2. I'll take credit for my successes but refuse blame for my failures.	b. lexical decision task
_____ 3. When something is easy to think of or to recall.	c. self-serving bias
_____ 4. To seek and focus on information that proves your working hypothesis.	d. confirmation bias
_____ 5. A test designed to measure whether stereotypes are activated or not.	e. scapegoat theory

Summary

Use the appropriate terms to complete each summary.

1. We may hold a stereotype about Icelanders as being stoic individuals because of the ______________________ of a particular image. When we are motivated to protect our own self-esteem or ego, we may blame out group members for our failures. ______________________ theory explains this tendency results in the development of negative feelings toward outgroup members. Other research suggests that we do not readily apply stereotypes, but instead interpret information in a stereotypic manner due to the ______________________.

Section 5: Overcoming Stereotypes, Reducing Prejudice

Snapshot

Americans have come a long way in reducing overt discrimination and providing equal opportunities to all individuals; however, research shows that America still has a long way to go to truly become a non-prejudicial society. Research by Devine has found that all people know stereotypes and have those stereotypes activated under certain conditions, but that non-prejudicial people make a conscious effort to override stereotypic thoughts. People may be motivated to override stereotypes because of a deeply held belief in equality and fairness or because they do not want to appear prejudicial to others.

Learning Objectives

- Explain why conscious override is important to prejudice.
- Describe how knowledge of prejudice might result in acting in a way opposite the prejudice.
- Describe how motives for overcoming prejudice influences behavior.
- Explain how contact and superordinate goals influence overcoming prejudice.

Summary

Use the appropriate terms to complete each summary.

1. Research has shown that it takes ______________________ to overcome prejudice and that after talking with a person of another race, individuals perform ______________________ on measures of ______________________.

2. Some individuals have an ______________________ motivation to respond without prejudice and tend to respond the same whether it is public or private. On the other hand, some individuals have an ______________________ motivation to respond without prejudice and may feel angered if they feel pressure to be politically correct.

Section 6: Impact of Prejudice on Targets

Snapshot

Prejudice and stereotypes can impact the targets of the prejudice and stereotypes through self-fulfilling prophecy and stereotype threat. Both of these mechanisms can result in negative stereotypes coming true for individuals that are stereotyped. Work by Crocker has also shown that stigma can have unexpected effects such as a buffering of self-esteem for those who are stigmatized.

Learning Objectives

- Compare and contrast self-fulfilling prophecy and self-defeating prophecy.
- Explain why African Americans have higher self-esteem, on average, than European Americans.
- Explain how stereotype threat impacts performance.

Understanding Terminology

Match the terms on the right to the definitions/examples on the left.

_____ 1. When an expectation comes true because of the behavior it generates.	a. self-fulfilling prophecy
_____ 2. When an expectation does not come true because of the behavior it generates.	b. self-defeating prophecy
_____ 3. When worry over confirming a negative stereotype impairs performance.	c. stereotype threat

Summary

Use the appropriate terms to complete each summary.

1. If a teacher expects you to perform poorly because of your family background, the teacher is likely to ________________________ differently toward you, thus generating ________________________ performance from you. This is called a ________________________ prophecy.

2. If I am a girl and I know that people think that girls cannot excel in difficult math classes, I may experience worry that I will ________________________ a negative stereotype about my group and this worry may interfere with my performance. This is called ________________________.

CHAPTER TEST

Multiple Choice Questions

1. Martha refuses to rent an apartment to an Arab-American. This is an example of ___
   a. homophobia.
   b. stereotyping.
   c. prejudice.
   d. discrimination.

2. I am a member of a fraternity on campus. I believe that members of my fraternity are all individuals with different beliefs, likes, and majors. However, I believe that members of other fraternities are all alike. This is an example of ___
   a. outgroup heterogeneity bias.
   b. outgroup homogeneity bias.
   c. stigma by association.
   d. social categorization.

3. I just do not like people from our rival school. This is an example of ___
   a. homophobia.
   b. stereotyping.
   c. prejudice.
   d. discrimination.

4. Steve thinks that most gay men are effeminate. He then meets Marc who is the starting linebacker on the college football team. What is Steve likely to think about gay men after meeting Marc?
   a. He is likely to think that his stereotype was wrong and he should change his views.
   b. He is likely to subtype Marc as an exception to the rule.
   c. He is likely to change his stereotype to think that most gay men are football players.
   d. None of the above are likely.

5. In a study conducted to examine if prejudice against Arabs would translate into discrimination, what did Bushman and Bonacci find?
a. They found that college students who were prejudiced against Arabs were no more likely or less likely to actually discriminate against Arabs.
b. They found that college students who were prejudiced were actually motivated to appear unprejudiced and thus were less discriminatory against Arabs than other students.
c. They found that college students who were prejudiced against Arabs were more likely to discriminate against Arabs.
d. They found that college students who were prejudiced against Arabs were likely to discriminate by not forwarding good news but did not discriminate when given a chance of forwarding bad news.

6. Many Israelis are friends with Palestinians. Yet, the two groups cannot form lasting peace. What concept best explains this quandary?
a. superordinate goals
b. contact hypothesis
c. discontinuity effect
d. minimal group effect

7. If a group of participants is divided on the basis of whether they overestimated or underestimated the number of beans in a jar, what is likely to happen?
a. Participants will show ingroup favoritism.
b. Participants will not show ingroup favoritism because the grouping is meaningless.
c. Participants will not show ingroup favoritism because there is no competition for resources.
d. Participants will not show ingroup favoritism because they have had interpersonal contact.

8. Which of the following is not an important condition that must be met for contact to reduce prejudice?
a. People must be of equal status.
b. People must desire to change their prejudicial attitudes.
c. People must be involved in positive interactions.
d. People must perceive the outgroup members to be typical of their group.

9. A motivational explanation for prejudice suggests that favoring one's own group can increase one's own ___ by virtue of being a member of an esteemed group.
a. wealth
b. power
c. friendship circle
d. self-esteem

10. Research by Janet Swim on gender stereotypes found that
a. gender stereotypes were wildly exaggerated.
b. gender stereotypes were inaccurate in content.
c. gender stereotypes tended to be accurate in content and degree.
d. both a and b

1. A person believes that members of group X tend to be stupid and polite. Which of these two stereotypes is more resistant to change?
a. stupid
b. polite
c. both would be easy to change with contradictory information
d. both would be difficult to change because stereotypes are hard to change

2. What theory explains why lynchings of blacks went up when cotton prices went down?
a. confirmation bias theory
b. realistic conflict theory
c. contact theory
d. scapegoat theory

3. Focusing on information that supports your expectations is called ___
a. expectancy theory.
b. confirmation bias.
c. self-fulfilling prophecy.
d. self-serving bias.

4. I live in a dorm in which 10% of the residents are international students. I fail my social psychology exam and blame it on international students because I feel they monopolize the study room. However, that same day, I ace my abnormal psychology exam and congratulate myself for doing a good job. What phenomenon am I illustrating?
a. expectancy theory
b. confirmation bias
c. self-fulfilling prophecy
d. self-serving bias

5. After responding to a public situation in a nonprejudicial manner, I become more prejudicial when in private. What type of motivation do I have?
a. internal motivation to respond without prejudice
b. external motivation to respond without prejudice
c. no motivation to appear nonprejudicial
d. motivation to show reverse discrimination

16. Which part of the mind says “stop” to prejudice?
a. duplex mind
b. automatic system
c. conscious system
d. equality part

17. Which of the following is a difference between prejudiced and nonprejudiced people?
a. Prejudiced people know more stereotypes.
b. Stereotypes become more activated in prejudiced people.
c. Prejudiced people use less conscious control to override stereotypes.
d. All of the above are true.

18. Professor Smith believes that women cannot excel in engineering. When Sally enrolls in his class, he never calls on her and provides her with little constructive feedback. As a result, Sally figures that she cannot improve her skills and changes her major. What is this an example of?
a. stereotype threat
b. self-esteem protection
c. self-fulfilling prophecy
d. self-defeating prophecy

19. According to research by Crocker, stigmatized individuals use three strategies to protect themselves from stigma. Which of the following is not one of these strategies?
a. work to eliminate the group level stigma
b. make social comparisons with people from their own group
c. attribute failure to discrimination and prejudice
d. judge themselves on characteristics that make them look good

20. White men playing basketball may worry about confirming the stereotype that white men cannot jump. If this worry interferes with their performance, they may be experiencing ____
a. stereotype threat.
b. self-esteem protection.
c. self-fulfilling prophecy.
d. self-defeating prophecy.

True or False Questions

T F 1. Simply sitting next to an overweight person can hurt a person's chance of being evaluated favorably.

T F 2. The derogatory word "fag" comes from the term "faggot" that means a bundle of wood to be set on fire.

T F 3. The Chewong of the Malay Peninsula have 12 words for competition.

T F 4. The Eagles and Rattlers became friends only after working on superordinate goals together.

T F 5. Stereotypes are always negative.

T F 6. Disagreement and conflict tend to encourage the use of stereotypes.

T F 7. People have either internal or external motivations to respond without prejudice, but not both.

T F 8. The jigsaw classroom is an effective tool for reducing prejudice among students.

T F 9. Some stigmatized individuals may withdraw from a particular demand rather than risk confirming a negative stereotype about one's group.

T F 10. A self-defeating prophecy is a prediction that ensures its failure by the behavior it generates.

Short Essay Questions

1. What are the ABCs of intergroup relations?

2. Describe three reasons why prejudice exists.

3. What is stereotype threat and why is it so insidious?

Suggested Readings

Christopher, A., & Mull, M. (2006). Conservative ideology and ambivalent sexism. *Psychology of Women Quarterly*, *30*(2), 223-230.

Klonis, S., Plant, E., & Devine, P. (2005). Internal and external motivation to respond without sexism. *Personality and Social Psychology Bulletin*, *31*(9), 1237-1249.

Osborne, J., & Walker, C. (2006). Stereotype threat, identification with academics, and withdrawal from school: Why the most successful students of colour might be most likely to withdraw. *Educational Psychology*, *26*(4), 563-577.

Oswald, D. (2005). Understanding anti-Arab reactions post-9/11: The role of threats, social categories, and personal ideologies. *Journal of Applied Social Psychology* *35*(9), 1775-1799.

Ratcliff, J., Lassiter, G., Markman, K., & Snyder, C. (2006). Gender differences in attitudes toward gay men and lesbians: The role of motivation to respond withou prejudice. *Personality and Social Psychology Bulletin*, *32*(10), 1325-1338.

Answer Key

Section 1

Understanding Terminology

1. h	8. e
2. l	9. k
3. j	10. i
4. f	11. g
5. c	12. d
6. n	13. b
7. a	14. m

Summary

1. categorize, ingroup, outgroup, prejudice, stereotype, discrimination
2. stigma by association, Arabs, obese individuals, homosexuals

Section 2

Understanding Terminology

1. h
2. f
3. e
4. c
5. b
6. d
7. a
8. g

Summary

1. ingroup favoritism, minimal group effect
2. competition, realistic conflict, superordinate, cooperation
3. contact, equal status, positive, typical

Section 3

Summary

1. kernel of truth, negative, positive

Section 4

Understanding Terminology

1. e
2. c
3. a
4. d
5. b

Summary

1. salience, scapegoat, confirmation bias

Section 5

Summary

1. self-regulation, poorer, self-regulation
2. internal, external

Section 6

Understanding Terminology

1. a
2. b
3. c

Summary

1. behave, poor, self-fulfilling
2. confirm, stereotype threat

Chapter Test

Multiple Choice

1. d (p. 403)
2. b (p. 405)
3. c (p. 403)
4. b (p. 403)
5. c (p. 406)
6. c (p. 414)
7. a (p. 412)
8. b (p. 417)
9. d (p. 418)
10. c (p. 420)
11. a (p. 421)
12. d (p. 421)
13. b (p. 423)
14. d (p. 421)
15. b (p. 428)
16. c (p. 425)
17. c (p. 426)
18. c (p. 430)
19. a (p. 433)
20. a (p. 434)

True or False

1. T (p. 408)
2. T (p. 409)
3. F (p. 415)
4. T (p. 413)
5. F (p. 420)
6. T (p. 422)
7. F (p. 427)
8. T (p. 428)
9. T (p. 435)
10. T (p. 431)

Short Essay

1. What are the ABCs of intergroup relations?

- Affect = prejudice
- Behavior = discrimination
- Cognition = stereotype

2. Describe three reasons why prejudice exists.

- Realistic group conflict – competition over scarce resources creates ingroup favoritism
- Ignorance – can be eliminated under certain conditions by intergroup contact
- Stereotypes as heuristics make our social world simpler
- Prejudice helps us rationalize the status quo
- Prejudice may allow us to maintain or boost our own self-esteem

3. What is stereotype threat and why is it so insidious?

- Stereotype threat occurs when an individual fears confirming a negative stereotype about their own group. This pressure of being worried about letting down the entire group can hurt performance. It is particularly insidious because often the best and brightest may leave domains in which there are negative stereotypes about their group.

CHAPTER 13 – SOCIAL INFLUENCE AND PERSUASION

CHAPTER REVIEW

Section 1: Two Types of Social Influence

Snapshot

People often conform to others' beliefs or behaviors. This can occur through normative influence or informational influence. Asch found that the fear of standing out as different from the group motivated people to conform to things that they privately did not accept as true. Sherif, using the autokinetic effect, showed that people also conform when they believe others have useful information. In this way, group norms develop.

Learning Objectives

- Compare and contrast normative and information influence.
- Define the autokinetic effect and tell why it is important to social psychology.
- Define group norms, private acceptance, and public compliance.

Understanding Terminology

Match the terms on the right to the definitions/examples on the left.

______ 1. Conforming to the group in order to be liked.	a. group norms
______ 2. Truly believing whatever you are conforming to.	b. normative influence
______ 3. Occurs when groups come to accept behaviors or beliefs as normal.	c. private acceptance
______ 4. Conforming to a group because you believe they have useful information.	d. public compliance
______ 5. Outwardly conforming, but not really believing.	e. autokinetic effect
______ 6. Utilized by Sherif to study group norm formation.	f. informational influence

Summary

Use the appropriate terms to complete each summary.

1. ________________________ often results in the development of group norms and tends to produce ________________________. On the other hand, ________________________ is about "going along to get along" and tends to produce ________________________, not a true change in beliefs or attitudes.

Section 2: Techniques of Social Influence

Snapshot

Many techniques that salespeople or scam artists use rely on principles such as commitment, consistency, and reciprocity. Other techniques take advantage of the phenomenon that rare things are more valuable. Finally, some techniques work at either capturing our attention to break our pre-formulated scripts or to disrupt our attention. Many of the people employing these techniques are hoping that the target will use their automatic mind and will not consciously process the information.

Learning Objectives

- Identify the techniques of social influence based in commitment and consistency (foot-in-the-door technique, low-ball technique, bait-and-switch technique, labeling technique, and legitimization-of-paltry-favors technique).
- Identify the techniques of social influence based on reciprocation (door-in-the-face technique, and that's-not-all technique).
- Identify the techniques of social influence based on scarcity.
- Identify the techniques of social influence based on capturing and disrupting attention (pique technique, disrupt-then-frame technique).

Understanding Terminology

Match the terms on the right to the definitions/examples on the left.

______ 1. Interrupting critical thinking and then giving a positive spin.
______ 2. E.g., first telling a person they are generous and then asking for money.
______ 3. First asking for something small and then asking for something larger.
______ 4. E.g., Would you volunteer your time? Even five minutes will help.
______ 5. Disrupting a refusal script by making a unique request.
______ 6. First getting someone to agree to one price and then adding in hidden costs.
______ 7. First asking for something very large and then making a smaller request.
______ 8. Makes an initial offer and then adds a bonus or extra discount before the first offer is either rejected or accepted.
______ 9. First getting someone interested with one offer and then saying it isn't available and providing a less attractive offer.

a. door-in-the-face-technique
b. low-ball technique
c. that's-not-all technique
d. bait-and-switch
e. pique technique
f. labeling technique
g. disrupt-then-reframe technique
h. foot-in-the-door technique
i. legitimization-of-paltry-favors technique

Summary

Use the appropriate terms to complete each summary.

1. One persuasive technique that relies on ________________________ is asking for a big request and then making a concession by asking for a smaller request. People feel the need to reciprocate the concession and are more likely to agree to the big request. This is called ________________________.

2. The ________________________ technique works by disrupting a person's ________________________ for behavior by capturing their attention with an unusual request.

3. Because most people think of themselves as ________________________ people, they are likely to give time or money if they are made to feel that a small amoun of assistance is okay. This is called the ________________________ technique.

Section 3: Persuasion

Snapshot

Many different variables influence whether a message is persuasive or not. For example, the source of the message is critically important. Is the source credible, likeable, or knowledgeable? The content of the message also matters. Is the message two-sided, frightening, or humorous? The audience is also important. What age are the audience members? Are they intelligent, motivated, distracted or concerned for their public image? Finally, this section discusses two routes to persuasion. One route is the thoughtful analytical route that relies on quality of arguments. The second route is automatic and does not rely on conscious thought or analytical reasoning.

Learning Objectives

- Describe the effect source credibility and likeability has on persuasion.
- Explain how covert communicators can influence health behaviors.
- Describe the effect of reason and emotion on persuasion.
- Describe the effect of revealing incriminating information (stealing thunder) has on persuasion.
- Describe the effect of fear on persuasiveness of a message, particularly with regard to sex.
- Describe the effect that repetition of a message has on persuasion.
- Describe how persuasion differs depending on audience intelligence, need for cognition, concern for public image, age, culture, belief about being a target and level of distraction.
- Explain how negative political campaigns illustrate bad being stronger than good.
- Explain the two routes to persuasion and when each is likely to be taken.
- Compare and contrast alpha and omega strategies of performance.

Understanding Terminology

Match the terms on the right to the definitions/examples on the left.

______ 1. E.g., I used to believe X, but I now think Y is the best.	a. impressionable years hypothesis
______ 2. Attempts to change another person's attitudes.	b. stealing thunder
______ 3. Seeing the same advertisement six times in a one-hour telecast may cause this.	c. persuasion
______ 4. How much something matters to your own life.	d. elaboration likelihood model
______ 5. Reducing the impact of damaging information by being the one to release it.	e. source
______ 6. Persuasion via the less thoughtful route.	f. peripheral route
______ 7. The idea that young people are more likely to yield to persuasion.	g. trustworthiness
______ 8. The person who is delivering the message.	h. self-efficacy
______ 9. People who like to think, analyze, and solve problems are high in this.	i. advertisement wear-out
______ 10. Attempting to persuade by increasing desirability.	j. omega strategies
______ 11. May help avoid advertisement wear out.	k. expertise
______ 12. A theoretical model that posits two routes to persuasion.	l. heuristic/systematic model
______ 13. People are listening to and understanding the message.	m. yielding
______ 14. Another theoretical model that states there are two ways to persuasion.	n. central route
______ 15. E.g. "I no longer remember who told me this, but…"	o. convert communicators
______ 16. Accepting the persuasive message.	p. repetition with variation
______ 17. Attempting to persuade by decreasing the psychological obstacles.	q. two-sided message
______ 18. Is the source being honest?	r. sleeper effect
______ 19. Persuasion via consideration of the arguments.	s. alpha strategies
______ 20. The extent of knowledge the source possesses.	t. personal relevance
______ 21. A message that presents both sides and then refutes opposing arguments.	u. receptivity

_____ 22. A belief in one's abilities to successfully do things. v. need for cognition

Summary

Use the appropriate terms to complete each summary.

1. Whenever you are engaged in trying to change another person's attitude, you are ttempting ________________________. The person delivering the message is called e ________________________ and is more likely to be successful if seen as a(n) ________________________ (knowing a lot) or ________________________ (being onest).

2. About ________________________ of all ads are humorous. In addition to using umor, sources may also rely on the emotion of ________________________, in which ________________________ levels seem more effective than ________________________ levels.

3. Two important aspects for a message to be persuasive include whether a person gets" it. This is called ________________________. However, "getting" it is not nough, the message must also produce ________________________ in order to be ffective.

4. The ________________________ mind has two systems and we can be ersuaded through either system. The ________________________ route relies on the oughtful approach to arguments, while the ________________________ route relies n the acceptance of peripheral cues.

Section 4: Resisting Persuasion

Snapshot

Knowing how persuasive messages work allows individuals to be better prepared to resist techniques. This section discusses several ways to resist appeals.

Learning Objectives

- Explain how attitude inoculation, forewarning, and stockpiled resources reduce persuasiveness of a message.
- Describe how to defend against persuasive techniques based on commitment and consistency, reciprocation, scarcity, capturing and disrupting attention, and social proof.

Understanding Terminology

Match the terms on the right to the definitions/examples on the left.

_____ 1. Adding to the appeal by stressing how few are available.	a. limited-number technique
_____ 2. Adding to the appeal by saying there is only a short time to benefit.	b. negative attitude change
_____ 3. Boomerang effect	c. fast-approaching-deadline technique

Summary

Use the appropriate terms to complete each summary.

1. Research has found that people can be ______________________ against persuasive messages, just as they can be against the flu. This works by building defenses against future persuasion attempts.

2. People are less likely to be influenced by messages if they have already made a ______________________ commitment to their position. Further research shows that we can resist the limited-number technique by asking ourselves, do I want the item because it is ______________________ or because of its own ______________________.

CHAPTER TEST

Multiple Choice Questions

1. Jesse is not sure where the entrance is to the large park she is going to for a concert. She notices that others are walking a certain direction. She decides to follow. What is this an example of?
   a. normative influence
   b. informational influence
   c. public compliance
   d. pique technique

2. Informational influence is to ___ as normative influence is to ____
   a. private acceptance; public compliance.
   b. autokinetic effect; public compliance.
   c. public compliance; private acceptance.
   d. Asch; Sherif.

What type of influence was probably at work in the Jonestown suicide?
a. informational
b. normative
c. neither a or b
d. both a and b

How does one dissenter effect overall group conformity?
a. Having one dissenter does not seem to be enough to change the pressure to conform.
b. If the dissenter is too extreme, he or she has no effect on group conformity.
c. People are more willing to stand up for what they believe if there is a dissenter in the group.
d. If the dissenter is moderate in his/her dissent, he or she has no effect on group conformity.

The foot-in-the-door technique and the labeling technique are based on ___
a. commitment and consistency.
b. reciprocity.
c. scarcity.
d. disrupting attention.

Which of the following techniques is based on reciprocity?
a. low-ball technique
b. door-in-the-face
c. pique
d. disrupt-then-reframe

A salesperson initially offers you a computer for $400 and then, before you agreed to buy it, he says he will throw in the printer and monitor at no additional cost. What technique is this salesperson using?
a. foot-in-the-door technique
b. labeling technique
c. low-ball technique
d. that's-not-all technique

On the day after Thanksgiving, a store advertises that they have DVD players for $12.99. However, once you get to the store, they are sold out and the only DVD player available is $79.99. What technique does this illustrate?
a. foot-in-the-door technique
b. labeling technique
c. low-ball technique
d. bait-and-switch technique

9. Which of the following approaches would make a person more likely to pay someone to shampoo their carpets?
a. The carpet cleaner says, "Would you like me to shampoo your carpets? I'll do it for $75? No wait; I can give you the rate of $65."
b. The carpet cleaner says, "Would you like me to shampoo your carpets? I have just lowered my prices from $75 to $65."
c. The carpet cleaner says, "Would you like me to shampoo your carpets? I'll do it for $65"
d. There is no difference in the options above, $65 is the price.

10. Johnny has a friend who he thinks has terrible taste in movies. This friend tells Johnny he should really see a particular movie. Johnny thanks him for the advice and plans to ignore the advice because his friend is not credible when it comes to movie advice. However, one month later, while in the movie rental store, Johnny comes across the movie and decides he should watch it. What construct best explains this scenario?
a. trustworthiness
b. growing credibility
c. sleeper effect
d. source effect

11. Which factor(s) adds to the persuasiveness of convert communicators?
a. They are seen as being committed and consistent.
b. They often appear to be similar to audience members.
c. They have enhanced credibility because they overcame their undesirable behavior.
d. All of the above add to the persuasiveness of convert communicators.

12. Which of the following statements is generally true about fear appeals?
a. Fear appeals usually do not work because they invoke too much arousal and distraction.
b. Fear appeals always work because fear is such a great motivator.
c. Fear appeals can be effective, as long as they do not produce too much fear.
d. Fear only works to persuade people to avoid certain behaviors, but does not work to persuade people to do things.

13. Repeating ads too often may result in _____, but this can be ameliorated by the use of _____
a. advertisement wear-out; repetition with variation.
b. burnout; humorous ads.
c. annoyance; humorous ads.
d. advertisement wear-out; fear appeals

4. People with high self-esteem or intelligence may show more ___ than ___ to persuasive messages.
   a. yielding; receptivity
   b. receptivity; yielding
   c. yielding; effect
   d. awareness; listening

5. If a beer ad with attractive bikini clad women sells more beer, what route to persuasion is most likely being used?
   a. personal relevance route
   b. motivated route
   c. central route
   d. peripheral route

6. What route to persuasion results in the most lasting attitude change?
   a. personal relevance route
   b. motivated route
   c. central route
   d. peripheral route

7. Which would be an example of an omega strategy?
   a. emphasize scarcity
   b. distract resistance
   c. engage a norm of reciprocity
   d. add incentives

8. What is it called when people do the exact opposite of what they are being persuaded to do?
   a. reversal effect
   b. negative attitude change
   c. self-efficacy effect
   d. forewarned effect

9. A banner that reads, "Blow-out Sale, only a few remaining" is using the ___ technique.
   a. low-balling
   b. foot-in-the-door
   c. limited-number
   d. fast-approaching-deadline

20. If an ad claims that a particular product is the most popular product, they are trying to sell it based on ___
    a. social proof.
    b. foot-in-the-door.
    c. limited-number.
    d. fast-approaching-deadline.

True or False Questions

T F 1. Conformity continues to go up as long as the group size goes up.

T F 2. Sherif used an illusion produced by eye movements to study informational influence.

T F 3. A confederate posing as a salesperson sold more Christmas cards when he said the price was 300 pennies than when he said $3.00

T F 4. People volunteered more time when they were asked to donate two hours directly than when first asked to make a huge commitment and then asked for just two hours.

T F 5. Messages that people don't perceive as persuasion attempts can be particularly persuasive because people let their guard down.

T F 6. Age and yielding to persuasion are positively correlated.

T F 7. When political campaigns are negative, voters lower their evaluations of both candidates.

T F 8. Virgins who saw emotionally powerful films showing the consequences of unprotected sex felt increased risk compared to virgins in the control group.

T F 9. Research has shown that resisting weak attacks on a position can actually increase defenses against later attacks.

T F 10. Depriving people of sleep makes them more resistant to persuasion.

Short Essay Questions

1. Describe the two routes to persuasion.

2. What are some of the important differences between Asch's line study and Sherif's autokinetic study?

3. How is the foot-in-the-door technique different from the door-in-the-face technique?

Suggested Readings

Aaker, J., & Lee, A. (2001). 'I' seek pleasures and 'we' avoid pains: The role of self-regulatory goals in information processing and persuasion. *Journal of Consumer Research*, *28*(1), 33-49.

Bloom, P., McBride, C., Pollak, K., Schwartz-Bloom, R., & Lipkus, I. (2006). Recruiting teen smokers in shopping malls to a smoking-cessation program using the foot-in-the-door technique. *Journal of Applied Social Psychology*, *36*(5), 1129-1144.

Dedobbeleer, N., Morissette, P., & Rojas-Viger, C. (2005). Social network normative influence and sexual risk-taking among women seeking a new partner. *Women & Health*, *41*(3), 63-82.

Meffert, M., Chung, S., Joiner, A., Waks, L., & Garst, J. (2006). The effects of negativity and motivated information processing during a political campaign. *Journal of Communication*, *56*(1), 27-51.

Neighbors, C., Lewis, M., Bergstrom, R., & Larimer, M. (2006). Being controlled by normative influences: Self-determination as a moderator of a normative feedback alcohol intervention. *Health Psychology*, *25*(5), 571-579.

Wheeler, S., Briñol, P., & Hermann, A. (2007). Resistance to persuasion as self-regulation: Ego-depletion and its effects on attitude change processes. *Journal of Experimental Social Psychology*, *43*(1), 150-156.

Answer Key

Section 1

Understanding Terminology

1.	b	4.	f
2.	c	5.	d
3.	a	6.	e

Summary

1. informational influence, private acceptance, normative influence, public compliance

Section 2

Understanding Terminology

1.	g	4.	i	7.	a
2.	f	5.	e	8.	c
3.	h	6.	b	9.	d

Summary

1. reciprocity, door-in-the-face technique
2. pique, script
3. helpful, legitimization-of-paltry-favors

Section 3

Understanding Terminology

1.	o	8.	e	15.	r	22.	h
2.	c	9.	v	16.	m		
3.	i	10.	s	17.	i		
4.	t	11.	p	18.	g		
5.	b	12.	l	19.	n		
6.	f	13.	u	20.	k		
7.	a	14.	d	21.	q		

Summary

1. persuasion, source, expert, trustworthy
2. 40%, fear, moderate, high
3. receptivity, yielding
4. duplex, central, peripheral

Section 4

Understanding Terminology

1. a
2. c
3. b

Summary

1. inoculated
2. public, scarce, merits

Chapter Test

Multiple Choice

1. b (p. 446)
2. a (p. 446)
3. d (p. 446)
4. c (p. 445)
5. a (p. 447)
6. b (p. 450)
7. d (p. 451)
8. d (p. 448)
9. a (p. 451)
10. c (p. 455)
11. d (p. 456)
12. c (p. 457)
13. a (p. 459)
14. b (p. 460)
15. d (p. 463)
16. c (p. 463)
17. b (p. 466)
18. b (p. 469)
19. c (p. 471)
20. a (p. 472)

True or False

1. F (p. 444)
2. T (p. 445)
3. T (p. 452)
4. F (p. 450)
5. T (p. 462)
6. F (p. 461)
7. T (p. 460)
8. T (p. 458)
9. T (p. 468)
10. F (p. 470)

Short Essay

1. Describe the two routes to persuasion.

- Central Route – relies on conscious analytical thought. People must be both motivated and capable of understanding for this route to work. If it works, it tend to produce lasting attitude change that is resistant to future persuasive appeals and predicts behavior.
- Peripheral route – require little mental effort and relies on peripheral cues such as speaker credibility or source attractiveness. If it results in attitude change, the change is usually temporary and vulnerable to subsequent persuasive appeals. It does not generally predict behavior.

2. What are some of the important differences between Asch's line study and Sherif's autokinetic study?

- Asch's line study had an easy to do task where people would stand out from a group of similar others if they did not conform. This created conformity due to normative influence. In other words, people conformed to be accepted by the group.
- Sherif's autokinetic study had a very ambiguous task in which participants looked to one another for cues on how to respond. Thus, their conformity was due to information influence and created a lasting group norm.

3. How is the foot-in-the-door technique different from the door-in-the-face technique?
   - The foot-in-the-door technique relies on people's motivation to appear committed and consistent. Thus, after first agreeing to a small request, people feel that in order to appear commitment and consistent, they must then agree to the larger request.
   - The door-in-the-face technique relies on people's belief that they are helpful and that they should reciprocate when someone does something for them. In this case, a large request is made. After being rejected, a smaller request is made which feels to the person like the requestor is giving them something by reducing the request, thus in order to reciprocate, the person then agrees to the smaller request.

CHAPTER 14 – GROUPS

CHAPTER REVIEW

Section 1: What Groups Are and Do

Snapshot

It is difficult to give just one definition for what it means to be a group. Groups tend to have a common identity, interact frequently, depend on one another, work toward common goals, and share common beliefs, values, and practices. Another important factor is the presence of an outgroup as a competitor.

Learning Objectives

- Define a group.
- Explain what makes a group feel united and what groups can do.
- Describe the tradeoff of diversity in groups.

Summary

Use the appropriate terms to complete each summary.

1. Technically, a group consists of ____________________ or more people who are doing or being something together. As social and cultural beings, we likely belong to groups because groups provide ____________________ to us. Because of our groups, we do not have to be ____________________ in how to do everything, instead we can ____________________.

Section 2: Groups, Roles, and Selves

Snapshot

Groups can become dangerous when deindividuation occurs and individuals lose a sense of self awareness and individuality. Marilyn Brewer has proposed optimal distinctiveness theory which argues that people have conflicting needs to be similar to group members and to be distinct from group members. Groups rely both on similarity and role differentiation.

Learning Objectives

- Define deindividuation and its potential effects.
- Explain optimal distinctiveness theory.

Summary

Use the appropriate terms to complete each summary.

1. The saying, "carried away by the group" means that a person was __________________. In other words they lose their __________________.

2. __________________ theory suggests that people struggle to balance being __________________ to group member and being __________________ from group members.

Section 3: Group Action

Snapshot

Social facilitation is the finding that people's dominant response is increased when in the presence of others. This can lead to better or poorer performance depending on the task and the individual. Another important construct is social loafing. This is the finding that people tend to put less effort into a task if a group is working together and their individual contributions cannot be distinguished. Group behavior is also seen in mob violence and in the commons dilemma.

Learning Objectives

- ❖ Explain social facilitation and the effect it has on performance.
- ❖ Describe how social facilitation works and how the bad apple effect relates.
- ❖ Describe the effect of others on eating.
- ❖ Define altruistic punishment and why it is important.
- ❖ Explain the conflicts present in the commons dilemma.
- ❖ Describe the effect of acceptance and rejection by groups on self-esteem.

Understanding Terminology

Match the terms on the right to the definitions/examples on the left.

______ 1. People work less when in a group compared to when alone.	a. social facilitation theory
______ 2. Worry over how others see your performance.	b. narcissists
______ 3. People are willing to sacrifice their own profits to punish people who cheat.	c. bad apple effect
______ 4. People who think highly of themselves and are constantly looking for praise.	d. altruistic punishment
______ 5. Shared resources often are not used in the most optimal way.	e. evaluation apprehension
______ 6. If one person does less than his/her share, others may imitate.	f. commons dilemma
______ 7. An audience leads to the dominant response.	g. dominant response
______ 8. A person's typical response.	h. social loafing

Summary

Use the appropriate terms to complete each summary.

1. If a person usually makes free throws during a basketball game, her performance will be __________________ with an audience present, but if she usually misses free throws, her performance will be __________________ with an audience present. This is because her __________________ is strengthened in the presence of others. This i called __________________.

2. __________________ occurs when people feel __________________ in a grou and do not feel individually __________________.

Section 4: How Groups Think

Snapshot

It seems like groups should be beneficial in most cases; however, the research has indicated that there are good and bad things about groups, although the good definitely outweighs the bad. This section discusses brainstorming, groupthink, and group polarization.

Learning Objectives

- Explain how brainstorming in groups is good for morale but poor for production of ideas.
- Describe the wisdom crowds have.
- Explain how groups can be helpful to memory.
- Explain how groupthink leads to poor decision making.
- Describe how committees can make bad decisions.
- Explain the risky shift and group polarization.

Understanding Terminology

Match the terms on the right to the definitions/examples on the left.

_____ 1. In certain situations, group members fail to think independently.	a. groupthink
_____ 2. Groups tend to take a more extreme position than the individuals would have.	b. transactive memory
_____ 3. When different individuals remember different pieces of information.	c. self-censorship
_____ 4. Keeping one's doubts or discouraging thoughts from the group	d. brainstorming
_____ 5. People enjoy this and believe that it works, but it does not produce better work.	e. risky shift
_____ 6. Taking bigger chances when in a group.	f. group polarization

Summary

Use the appropriate terms to complete each summary.

1. If people get together at a conference supporting gun control, most participants vill become ____________________ supportive of gun control. This is called ____________________.

2. People believe that ____________________ is beneficial and produces excellent esults, but in reality a group of people produce better quality ideas when each is vorking ____________________.

3. ____________________ results in members of the group thinking alike and failing o consider alternatives. It is likely occurring if there is pressure toward ____________________ and a ____________________ of doubts. Other signs include an ____________________ (the belief that nothing can go wrong), having a sense of moral ____________________, and a tendency to ____________________ opponents.

Section 5: Power and Leadership

Snapshot

A lot of work is still needed to understand leadership and power. Power is defined as one person's control over another person. Power has many different effects on leaders. One important aspect to power is that is removes inhibitions while the lack of power makes people feel more inhibited.

Learning Objectives

- Describe the importance of leadership.
- Define power and the effect it has on leaders and followers.
- Describe legitimizing myths and how they support the power of a leader.

Summary

Use the appropriate terms to complete each summary.

1. __________________ is important to corporate success as seen in a study that found that high-performing executives added an average of __________________ to the value of their company.

2. Power can seem __________________ in that people often strive to increase their own power. Unfortunately, more powerful leaders (in terms of objective power) tend to treat their workers __________________. People with power are more likely to be motivated by __________________ while people lacking power focus more on __________________.

3. __________________ help powerful people keep their power by explaining why they deserve the power.

CHAPTER TEST

Multiple Choice Questions

1. Which of the following is likely the most cohesive group?
   a. People waiting at a bus stop.
   b. People in a movie theatre watching the same movie.
   c. Co-workers working together to develop a business strategy.
   d. People who live in France.

2. Evolutionary psychologists believe we evolved to form groups to be able to ___
   a. effectively build shelter.
   b. effectively compete against outgroups.
   c. effectively gather food.
   d. effectively raise children.

3. Trick-or-treaters wearing masks are more likely to experience ___ than trick-or-treaters who are identifiable.
   a. self-awareness
   b. evaluation apprehension
   c. deindividuation
   d. group think

4. Who or what creates the roles that people occupy within a group?
   a. the system
   b. the individual
   c. the leaders
   d. all of the above

5. If a person feels very similar to everyone else in the group, according to optimal distinctiveness theory, what will the person desire?
   a. to support the group
   b. to find even more commonality
   c. to distinguish self from the group
   d. to leave the group

6. Rebecca is a very good ping pong player. She is invited to the student union to play with a friend. There are a lot of people in the union who stop to watch the ping pong game. How does Rebecca play?
   a. She plays the same as when playing without an audience.
   b. She plays even better than usual.
   c. She plays worse than usual because the audience makes her nervous.
   d. There is not enough information to predict her performance.

7. What animal did Zajonc use when studying how audiences infuence maze running?
   a. white mice
   b. rats
   c. cockroaches
   d. dogs

8. Narcissists tend to perform best under what condition?
   a. When others are watching
   b. When there are important individual rewards at stake
   c. When others are relying on the performance
   d. both a and b

9. Social loafing is also known as the ___
   a. free rider problem.
   b. lazy person syndrome.
   c. deindividuation.
   d. bad apple effect.

10. Which of the following is an example of altruistic punishment?
    a. punishing one person to help another person
    b. donating money to help build the community jail for crooks
    c. withholding punishment from someone who deserve it
    d. all of the above are good examples.

11. According to Postmes and Spears, what is the biggest predictor of aggression?
    a. media
    b. family upbringing
    c. social norms
    d. accountability

12. What ideology worked to eliminate greed by making everything shared property?
    a. democracy
    b. communism
    c. fascism
    d. socialism

13. In graduate school, I become friends with a group of people who believe very strongly in a woman's right to choose. I also believe this. After talking about the idea, my views are likely to become ___
a. more extreme.
b. less extreme.
c. stay the same.
d. less important to me.

14. In the board meeting, I think to myself, "This is a very bad idea." However, I decide not to say anything because I do not want to upset the group. What is this called?
a. group polarization
b. illusion of invulnerability
c. self-censorship
d. a sense of moral authority

15. Which of the following is a sign of groupthink?
a. illusion of invulnerability
b. an appearance of unanimous agreement
d. a sense of moral authority
d. all of the above

16. Sheela and her friends want to make and send birthday cards to family members. One friend remembers the birthdays. Another friend remembers the addresses. A third friend remembers to buy construction paper . Sheela remembers where the scissors are kept. Together, they have all the information they need. What is this called?
a. groupthink
b. transactive memory
c. brainstorming
d. group polarization

17. Recent research has found that leaders tend to be ___
a. decisive.
b. competent.
c. honest.
d. all of the above

18. Managers without objective power tended to ___
a. give commands.
b. make threats.
c. make promises.
d. propose goals.

19. "What can you do for me?" is to "What can I do for you?" as ___ is to ___
    a. high power; low power.
    b. low power; high power.
    c. leadership; power.
    d. power; leadership.

20. The statement, "All people with purple eyes are unmotivated" may be a way to ___ discrimination against people with purple eyes, and thus maintains the power of people without purple eyes.
    a. legitimize
    b. end
    c. lower
    d. raise

True or False Questions

T F 1. Having diversity is always beneficial to group functioning.

T F 2. Emotionally powerful experiences can make a group of people feel more cohesive.

T F 3. Roles exist independently of the individual.

T F 4. Henry Ford was the first to realize how important it was to have role specialization.

T F 5. We eat more when with friends and family because we spend more time at the table.

T F 6. Social loafing may occur in part because people do not want to be the sucker.

T F 7. Social acceptance impacts self-esteem more than social-rejection.

T F 8. Eight people working individually produce more ideas than eight people working as a team.

T F 9. If you average 400 people's guesses on how much snow there will be this winter in Wisconsin, the average is probably better than if you picked just one person who studied climatology and asked him/her to guess.

T F 10. When playing blackjack, people with low power were more likely to want more cards.

Short Essay Questions

1. Describe social facilitation theory.

2. When are groups likely to suffer from groupthink? What are the symptoms of groupthink?

3. What are the five crucial effects that power has on the powerful?

Suggested Readings

Barclay, P. (2006). Reputational benefits for altruistic punishment. *Evolution and Human Behavior*, *27*(5), 325-344.

O'Gorman, R., Wilson, D., & Miller, R. (2005). Altruistic punishing and helping differ in sensitivity to relatedness, friendship, and future interactions. *Evolution and Human Behavior*, *26*(5), 375-387.

Price, K., Harrison, D., & Gavin, J. (2006). Withholding inputs in team contexts: Member composition, interaction processes, evaluation structure, and social loafing. *Journal of Applied Psychology*, *91*(6), 1375-1384.

Rietzschel, E., Nijstad, B., & Stroebe, W. (2006). Productivity is not enough: A comparison of interactive and nominal brainstorming groups on idea generation and selection. *Journal of Experimental Social Psychology*, *42*(2), 244-251.

Suedfeld, P. (2004). Decision-making in Great Britain during the Suez crisis: Small groups and a persistent leader. *Political Psychology*, *25*(5), 817-820.

Answer Key

Section 1

Summary

1. two, benefits, experts, specialize

Section 2

Summary

1. deindividuated, self awareness
2. Optimal distinctiveness, similar, distinct

Section 3

Understanding Terminology

1. h
2. e
3. d
4. b
5. f
6. c
7. a
8. g

Summary

1. better, poorer, dominant response, social facilitation
2. social loafing, submerged, accountable

Section 4

Understanding Terminology

1. a
2. f
3. b
4. c
5. d
6. e

Summary

1. more, group polarization
2. brainstorming, individually
3. Groupthink, conformity, self-censorship, illusion of invulnerability, superiority, underestimate

Section 5

Summary

1. Leadership, 25 million
2. addictive, poorer, rewards, punishments
3. legitimizing myths

Chapter Test

Multiple Choice

1. c (p. 480)
2. b (p. 481)
3. c (p. 483)
4. a (p. 484)
5. c (p. 485)
6. b (p. 486)
7. c (p. 487)
8. d (p. 487)
9. a (p. 487)
10. b (p. 490)
11. d (p. 490)
12. b (p. 491)
13. a (p. 497)
14. c (p. 496)
15. d (p. 496)
16. b (p. 495)
17. d (p. 499)
18. d (p. 500)
19. a (p. 501)
20. a (p. 503)

True or False

1. F (p. 482)
2. T (p. 481)
3. T (p. 484)
4. F (p. 483)
5. T (p. 488)
6. T (p. 489)
7. F (p. 492)
8. T (p. 493)
9. T (p. 494)
10. F (p. 502)

Short Essay

1. Describe social facilitation theory.

- The presence of others results in greater arousal. That arousal causes a person's dominant response to be strengthened. Easy tasks become easier and difficult tasks become more difficult.

2. When are groups likely to suffer from groupthink? What are the symptoms of groupthink?

- Antecedents to group think include: 1) a lot of similarity and a sense of unity, 2) a directive leader, 3) isolation from opposing ideas, and 4) members believe the group is special or elite.
- The symptoms of group think include: 1) pressure toward conformity, 2) an appearance of unanimity because disagreement is suppressed, 3) the belief that nothing can possible go wrong, 4) a belief in the moral superiority or goodness of the group, and 5) a tendency to think of themselves as superior thus underestimating opponents.

3. What are the five crucial effects that power has on the powerful?

- It feels good to be powerful
- It focuses people on rewards
- It changes the way people think about relationships
- It makes people rely more on automatic thinking and less on analytical thinking
- It removes a person's inhibitions to action

APPLICATION MODULE A – CONSUMER BEHAVIOR

MODULE REVIEW

Learning Objectives

- Explain the various reasons why individual buy products.
- Describe the decision process in buying a product.
- Explain the environmental influences on purchasing.
- Define brand loyalty and explain why it is important.
- Describe the consumption process.
- Describe the effect of cash versus credit on purchasing behavior.
- Describe how purchase perception change and what affects these perceptions over time.
- Explain how consumption today is different from consumption in previous decades.
- Explain the effect of time poverty on buying behavior.
- Describe the dark side of consumption, including addiction, product misuse, and shrinkage.
- Explain how needs for sex are satisfied (or created) on the internet and the danger of this.
- Describe the options in the post-consumption process.

MODULE TEST

Multiple Choice Questions

1. Maslow described five levels of need. Of the following, which is the lowest?
   a. safety needs
   b. self-actualization needs
   c. esteem needs
   d. belonging and love needs

2. Johanah, a young woman, sees a commercial in which a woman is portrayed as a mother and homemaker. Based on past research, which of the following is likely to be true?
   a. She will say she is not interested in the product being advertised.
   b. She will reject the idea of a stereotyped woman and state her preference to be independent.
   c. She will say she prefers careers with less mathematics.
   d. She will say she prefers people to fulfill gender roles.

3. Typically, who do advertisers consider the "right" consumers?
a. wealthy women over 40
b. upper middle class people between 20-40
c. upper middle class people between 30-50
d. wealthy men over 40

4. Which of the following is true about sounds and buying patterns?
a. Super market sales go up 18% when slower music is played.
b. Wine shoppers buy more expensive wine when classical music is being played.
c. Shoppers looking at athletic shoes are more likely to buy when there is a basketball game on in the store.
d. Sound does not effect buying behavior.

5. What is it called when you buy something because you want others to know you own the product?
a. product misuse
b. usage error
c. "show-off" buying
d. conspicuous consumption

6. If your company just created a brand new cell phone model, which of the following names would be best for selling the product?
a. bilush
b. balush
c. badlush
d. belosh

7. Which of the following is true about the awareness of death and consumer behavior?
a. People reminded of death become more optimistic about their finances.
b. People reminded of death become less optimistic about their finances.
c. Being reminded of death is unrelated to consumer behavior.
d. People are more likely to save their money after being reminded of death.

8. Because of a feeling of ____, many people are buying products that help them multi-task.
a. frustration
b. time poverty
c. polychronic fatigue
d. time warp

9. My mother loves to go to yard sales or garage sales. She is participating in ___

a. narcissistic love.
b. environmental shrinkage.
c. lateral cycling.
d. product misuse.

0. Leticia has recently joined a band. The band did not have enough money to buy drums. Instead, Leticia purchased metal trash cans to substitute for drums. This is an example of ___

a. lateral cycling.
b. shrinkage.
c. product misuse.
d. polychromic behavior.

Short Essay Question

. Based on the material presented, what strategies might you employ if you were opening a store that wanted to sell expensive and fashionable scarves?

Answer Key

Module Test

Multiple Choice

1. a (p. A3)
2. c (p. A4)
3. b (p. A4)
4. b (p. A5)
5. d (p. A11)
6. a (p. A6)
7. a (p. A11)
8. b (p. A13)
9. c (p. A16)
10. c (p. A15)

Short Essay

1. Based on the material presented, what strategies might you employ if you were opening a store that wanted to sell expensive and fashionable scarves?

- You may try a number of strategies including manipulating the sound, the produc names, and ideas for misuse. In your answer expand on all of these strategies.

APPLICATION MODULE B – HEALTH

MODULE REVIEW

Learning Objectives

- Define health.
- Define stress.
- Compare and contrast the models of stress: fight-or-flight, general adaptation syndrome, cognitive appraisal model, tend-and-befriend.
- Describe the coping process.
- Explain the models that help us increase healthy behaviors (health belief model, theory of planned behavior, transtheoretical model).
- Describe how social psychology can help us increase safe sex practices.
- Describe how social psychology can help us foster healthy eating.
- Explain the social psychological factors that affect perception and treatment of illness.

MODULE TEST

Multiple Choice Questions

1. Sally is about to give a presentation in her research methods class. Based on this information, what can we say about her level of stress?
   a. It is very high, as giving a presentation is always stressful.
   b. It is low, as it is only a presentation in front of classmates.
   c. It is probably high, but not as high as it could be.
   d. It is impossible to know without knowing more about Sally.

2. If our homeostasis has been upset, we have experienced ___
   a. poor health.
   b. stress.
   c. fight or flight response.
   d. a positive event.

3. When women experience stress, their response may be ___ while men are more likely to respond with ___
   a. tend and befriend; withdraw and isolate.
   b. approach and cope; withdraw and isolate.
   c. tend and befriend; fight or flight.
   d. approach and cope; fight or flight.

4. I am failing my psychobiology class. I need to earn an A on the final to pass. In order to cope with this stress, I form a study group and make a specific schedule of what I will study when. This would be called ___ coping.
a. emotion-focused
b. problem-focused
c. avoidant
d. passive

5. Which of the following is not a component of the health belief model?
a. ease of behavior
b. consequences of the behavior
c. beliefs about the effectiveness of the behavior
d. social norms for the behavior

6. What is the first stage of behavior change according to the transtheoretical model?
a. action
b. contemplation
c. precontemplation
d. maintenance

7. One of the first successful attempts to change college students' behavior regarding condom use relied on a basic social psychological theory. Which theory did they use?
a. attribution theory
b. cognitive dissonance
c. attribution theory
d. theory of planned behavior

8. Frances believes that she is going to get sick after flying in an airplane. The day after flying she notices her throat is scratchy and that her body aches. She is likely to believe she is getting sick because of the ___ bias.
a. confirmation
b. illness
c. coping
d. attribution

9. Which personality factor(s) is (are) associated with the reporting of more physical symptoms?
a. high in anxiety
b. high in neuroticism
c. a and b
d. none of the above

10. How a person interprets a stressful event is called the person's ___
    a. coping.
    b. action.
    c. personality.
    d. appraisal.

Short Essay Question

1. Using the theory of planned behavior, propose an intervention to change people's smoking behavior.

Answer Key

Module Test

Multiple Choice

1. d (p. B2)
2. b (p. B4)
3. c (p. B6)
4. b (p. B7)
5. d (p. B8)
6. c (p. B10)
7. b (p. B11)
8. a (p. B14)
9. c (p. B15)
10. d (p. B5)

Short Essay

1. Using the theory of planned behavior, propose an intervention to change people's smoking behavior.

- To answer this question, you would propose an intervention that would aim to change people's attitudes, perception of subjective norms, and perceived contro A change in these factors should change a person's intention toward smoking behavior. According to the model, behavioral intention translates into behavior.

APPLICATION MODULE C – LAW

MODULE REVIEW

Learning Objectives

- Describe how eyewitness memory can be adversely affected by estimator and system variables.
- Contrast the various line-up procedures and identify the procedures more prone to error.
- Describe the effect an eyewitness has on jury decision making (persuasiveness).
- Explain the terms associated with juries and jury selection, including venire, voir dire, challenge for cause, peremptory challenge.
- Explain social psychologists contribution to jury selection.
- Describe how juries on capital cases may be different from other juries.
- Describe the effect of pretrial publicity on court decisions.
- Describe the tradeoff of convicting an innocent person versus protecting victims.

MODULE TEST

Multiple Choice Questions

1. What is it called if a witness fails to pick out the suspect in a target-present lineup?
a. hit
b. incorrect rejection
c. false identification
d. correct rejection

2. Variables such as race of the suspect, lighting at the scene, and witness confidence are ___ that may increase or decrease eyewitness accuracy.
a. independent variables
b. dependent variables
c. system variables
d. estimator variables

3. Which of the following statements is true?
a. It is easier to make an accurate eyewitness identification if the suspect has a distinctive face.
b. It is easier to make an accurate eyewitness identification if the witness had a longer exposure of the culprit's face.
c. Eyewitnesses have a difficult time making an accurate identification if the suspect was wearing sunglasses during the event but not in the lineup.
d. All of the above statements are true.

4. The association between confidence of identification and accuracy of identification can be improved by ___
a. asking witnesses to generate hypotheses about why their identification may be wrong before you ask them to estimate their confidence.
b. asking witnesses to generate hypotheses about why their identification is probably correct before you ask them to estimate their confidence.
c. thanking them for their cooperation in the investigation before you ask them to estimate their confidence.
d. reminding them of the importance of justice in a society before you ask them to estimate their confidence.

5. What is it called when the police officers present a witness with a lineup of people who they know are all innocent?
a. accuracy check lineup
b. simultaneous lineup
c. blank lineup
d. sequential lineup

6. Research has found that having an eyewitness has a remarkable influence on the willingness of juries to convict. In one study, it was found that having an eyewitness resulted in convictions 72% of the time. In this study, if the witness admitted that he had terrible vision and did not have his glasses on, the jury convicted ___ of the time.
a. 55%
b. 68%
c. 22%
d. 5%

7. What is it called when the judge and attorneys question potential jurors looking for bias?
a. venire
b. challenge for cause
c. voir dire
d. peremptory challenge

8. Which of the statements is true about women jurors and conviction rates?
a. Women are more likely than men to convict in rape cases.
b. Women are more likely than men to convict in child sexual abuse cases.
c. Women are less likely than men to convict in cases in which a woman is accused of killing her abusive husband.
d. All of the above are true.

▪. What type of attitudes are the best predictors of verdicts?
a. behavior specific attitudes
b. general attitudes
c. traditional attitudes
d. well-informed attitudes

0. What strategy appears to be effective in reducing the bias of pre-trial publicity?
a. providing jurors information that the media did not have
b. specific instructions to the jury to disregard information from the media
c. change of venue
d. continuance

;hort Essay Question

. What are estimator and system variables? Describe two of each and how they effect yewitness accuracy.

Answer Key

Module Test

Multiple Choice

1. b (p. C3)
2. d (p. C3)
3. d (p. C4)
4. a (p. C5)
5. c (p. C6)
6. b (p. C8)
7. c (p. C10)
8. d (p. C11)
9. a (p. C11)
10. c (p. C13)

Short Essay

1. What are estimator and system variables? Describe two of each and how they influence eyewitness accuracy.

- Estimator variables – variables that are not controlled by the criminal justice system and may influence eyewitness accuracy.
  - Characteristics of culprit and eyewitness, conditions at the crime scene
- System variables – variable that are controlled by the criminal justice system ar may influence eyewitness accuracy.
  - Instructions given to witness, lineup procedure, choice of foils.

APPLICATION MODULE D – ENVIRONMENT

MODULE REVIEW

Learning Objectives

- Describe the environmental problems we are currently facing.
- Describe the barriers to solving the environmental problems we are facing.
- Explain the tragedy of the commons.
- Define density and crowding and the effect it has on individuals.
- Define territory and personal space.
- Describe how humans are affected by the ambient environment, specifically by weather and climate, noise, and pollution.
- Describe the current situation with regard to scarcity of natural resources and what we can do about that issue.
- Describe the effect of disasters before, during, and after the disaster.
- Describe how social psychology can be used to help save the environment.
- Explain how environmental inaction (bad) can be stronger than environmental action (good).

MODULE TEST

Multiple Choice Questions

1. What is the missing hero trap?
a. The missing hero trap is when no one stands up for the environment.
b. The missing hero trap is when protectors of the environment are jailed for speaking up.
c. The missing hero trap is when information is withheld about the environment from people who are affected by it.
d. The missing hero trap is a video game where children learn about how to be a hero to the environment.

2. What is it called when destructive behavior only harms the person performing the behavior?
a. one-person trap
b. individual good-collective bad trap
c. tragedy of the commons
d. missing hero trap

3. Crowding is a subjective feeling that occurs when which of the following is true?
a. attributing arousal to the presence of other people
b. feeling that other people are preventing you from achieving objectives
c. feeling that one does not have control over staying or leaving the situation.
d. all of the above can turn density into crowding

4. Paula is speaking with a close friend. How much distance is probably between Paula and her friend?
a. less than 1 ½ feet
b. between 1 ½ and 4 feet
c. between 4 feet and 12 feet
d. more than 12 feet

5. On a crowded beach, Paul lays out his beach towel. He expects others to respect that they should not step on his towel. This is an example of ___
a. cognitive control.
b. territoriality.
c. space control.
d. prompts.

6. In their study, what did Glass and Singer find in terms of the effect of noise on task performance?
a. Volume was the most important variable.
b. Perceived control was the most important variable.
c. The presence of others was the most important variable.
d. All of the above were important in this study.

7. According to the module, what has been the most effective way to encourage people to conserve energy?
a. prompts in the environment
b. education
c. encouraging people to make public commitments
d. scare tactics

8. People often ignore warnings of possible natural disasters because they believe they can control their own outcomes. What is this called?
a. illusory correlation
b. control bias
c. illusion of control
d. cognitive dissonance

9. What is a hypocrisy induction?
   a. Effecting change by pointing out the inconsistencies between a person's own action and public attitudes.
   b. Effecting change by encouraging trust and communication among all parties.
   c. Joining a new organization which has bylaws against one's own values.
   d. Being a hypocrite.

10. Designing a new cell phone to be used for 18 months is an example of ___
    a. sensory overload.
    b. product control.
    c. planned obsolescence.
    d. hypocrisy induction.

Short Essay Question

1. Using concepts from social psychology, develop a plan to encourage college students to recycle more.

Answer Key

Module Test

Multiple Choice

1. c (p. D3)
2. a (p. D3)
3. d (p. D4)
4. b (p. D5)
5. b (p. D6)
6. b (p. D8)
7. c (p. D9)
8. c (p. D11)
9. a (p. D14)
10. c (p. D15)

Short Essay

1. Using concepts from social psychology, develop a plan to encourage college students to recycle more.

- ❖ A number of different approaches could be used. Possible concepts to apply include targeting specific attitudes, providing feedback, encouraging communication and public commitment, and using a hypocrisy induction.